Flag N

shortening
course

Flag N
over Flag X

committee boat
on station at the
finishing line

race postponed

Flag L

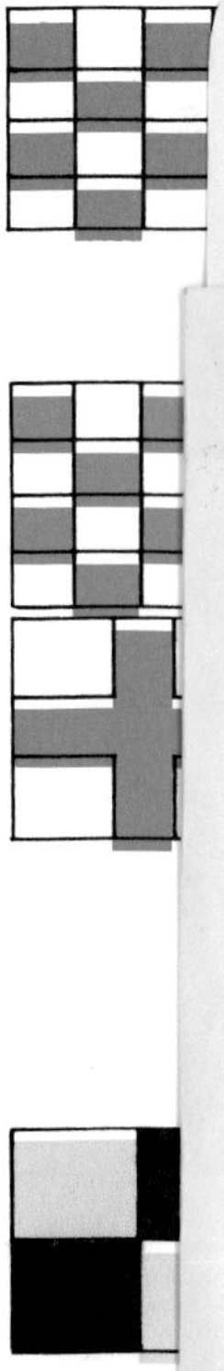

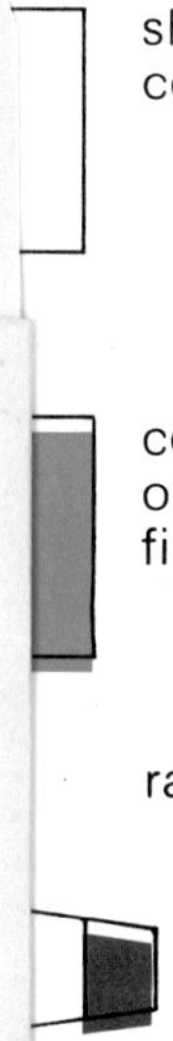

T

SAILBOARD RACING

Rainer Gutjahr

NAUTICAL BOOKS
MACMILLAN LONDON

Copyright © Delius Klasing and Co 1980
English language translation © Macmillan London Ltd 1981
Translated by Barbara Webb

This edition first published in Great Britain 1981 by
NAUTICAL BOOKS
Macmillan London Limited
4 Little Essex Street, London WC2R 3LF

Associated companies in Auckland, Dallas,
Delhi, Dublin, Hong Kong, Johannesburg,
Lagos, Manzini, Melbourne, Nairobi,
New York, Singapore, Tokyo, Washington
and Zaria

Reprinted 1983

Printed in Hong Kong

British Library Cataloguing in Publication Data

Gutjahr, Rainer
    Sailboard racing.
    1. Windsurfing
    I. Title   II. Das ist Regatta – Surfen. *English*
    797.1'24   GV811.63.W56

    ISBN 0-333-32213-4

Contents

Introduction

When people start to learn how to boardsail, they become so fascinated and enthusiastic that almost all of them take up the sport seriously. This is just what happened to me in the summer of 1972 when I stood on a board for the first time. The thrill of speed, and the wish to improve, drove me to sail in ever stronger winds, to learn to handle the board more efficiently, and to manage not to fall into the water so often. Although I had not consciously been comparing my performance with that of others, from the start I had been preparing myself for competition. Then, when my friends bought boards too, we each tried to beat, tack and gybe better than the others, and soon found that our board handling and manoeuvring could be considerably improved. We also discovered that the same tactics could be used as when racing in dinghies and catamarans.

Sailboard racing has now developed into an international sport, which is of ever-increasing importance to the manufacturers of sailboards and accessories both for comparing their products and for publicity purposes. The races have become exciting and tense, with the competitors often soaked in sweat after a race in light airs, owing to nervous tension and unremitting concentration; in fresh winds, they are sometimes utterly exhausted. If you ask them why they have decided to take up racing, their answers vary; some say, just to take part and to learn how to race, or to prove themselves by

being successful, or to concentrate on something completely different; others enjoy making new friends who share their interests, and the companionship of meeting almost every weekend for racing.

My main reason is that taking part in races enables me continuously to compare both my own performance and that of my sailboard and gear with those of others. Then again, there is the stimulus of trying to sail just that little bit faster than everyone else by using new ideas and better tactics when enjoying a healthy sport that is not dangerous.

I like to compare sailboard racing with chess. During a race there are very many alternative moves which the boardsailer may make, and they depend on the actions of other competitors and on wind and weather conditions. In order to profit, he needs to be able to anticipate quickly all the possible situations that could arise, and to handle his board skilfully and speedily when circumstances change.

Those who boardsail purely for pleasure spend most of the time reaching. It is only when racing that you are forced to beat to windward and to run, the points of sailing which, from the very first sail onwards, are the most difficult. Racing therefore improves the sailing skills of even good boardsailors, and enables them to get still more pleasure from their sport. Virtually everybody has an inner urge to improve, and the boardsailors who do

not race, for whom the greatest excitement and challenge is to plane over the water at maximum speed, continually attempt to improve their skills so that they can sail in ever stronger winds.

The aim of this book is to explain to the experienced boardsailor how a race is run, and to give him a chance of winning by advising him how to prepare his board and making suggestions on what tactics to use.

Just before the start of a Windsurfer race.

Requirements for racing

The first question that a competitively minded boardsailor who intends to take up racing asks is: In what class should I start racing? This is decided mainly by the type of board he owns, and the country in which he will race. On the continent races are held for a number of different classes, and although in Britain racing has been confined mainly to the Windsurfer and the open boardsailing classes there is an increase on the number of other designs racing as a class, for example the Sea Panther, the Dufour Wing, and the sailboard chosen by the IYRU for the 1984 Olympics, the Windglider.

Initially it is best to race in a relatively small fleet, preferably in waters which are familiar. Many boardsailing clubs run races especially for novices, and these are particularly suitable for those wanting to learn to race. Often the boardsailor is not required to be a member of the club or of a class association when entering for a novice race, but if he intends to take part frequently in sailboard races he should join the appropriate class association, or a sailing or sailboard club.

A good knowledge of the IYRU Racing Rules, many of which are quoted in this book, is also essential. Sailboard races are run along the same lines as races for sailing boats, and the same racing rules apply. A series consists of a number of races, each of which is won by a competitor whose completes a prescribed course by sailing from the start, round specific marks, to the finish in the shortest time. In order to win he has to choose the best route and sail at the highest possible speed. Chapters 1 and 2 set out how to achieve maximum board speed, while Chapter 4 explains how the shortest and fastest route should be selected. It must be said from the first, however, that the shortest route is not necessarily the fastest. The effect of tidal streams, currents, differences in wind speed and wind direction are so diverse that this subject has to be considered almost scientfically.

In a one design class, such as the Windsurfer, virtually identical boards compete against each other. Competition is keen because the class measurement rules are strict, and minor differences in speed result from sailing technique and racing tactics. In open class racing, on the other hand, performance is affected more by the differences in design and equipment of the various makes of sailboards taking part. Open races provide the opportunity for an owner to race a board he has designed himself, or one that he has altered or strengthened in some way to increase speed.

In all classes, rules limit size and specify what equipment may be used. In a tightly controlled class the rules are extremely strict, and this results in greater conformity of boards and equipment.

The start of a Mistral race.

1 Equipment for racing

The hull

Sailing techniques and tactics have reached a very high standard in the last few years and, to be among the leaders today, it is absolutely essential to use racing equipment that is at least as good as that of other competitors. Depending on the class, there are a number of possible ways of making a sailboard perform better and faster.

The first essential is to have a fast hull, which must be of suitable shape and construction for the conditions in which it will mainly be used. The sailboards that are available on the market can be broadly divided into two types:

- Those whose shape has been developed from surfboards; they have flat bottoms and curve upwards considerably at the bow.
- Those developed from boats and sailing dinghies; they have a slightly veed bow and a rounded or veed bottom.
- The sailing characteristics of these two basic types differ. In the case of flat boards with blunt bows, resistance to forward motion is high but, at high speeds, they are lifted and plane on the flat underwater surface, so providing a stable platform for the boardsailer. Given a suitably sized skeg, directional stability is good to very good when beam reaching, broad reaching and running. When the board is tilted and one side is immersed, the buoyancy resulting from the considerable volume of the relatively deep sides makes for stability when tacking, gybing and altering course.

Flat-bottomed and rounded hulls.

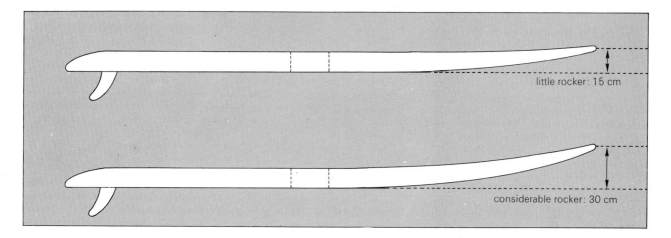

little rocker: 15 cm

considerable rocker: 30 cm

Boards with rounded or veed bottoms and sharper bows have a very much longer waterline length compared with their overall length. Just as with sailing boats, the longer the waterline length the greater the speed and this, combined with lower resistance to forward motion, means that they are faster than the flat-bottomed boards in the lower speed range. However there is very little increase in submerged volume when the boat tilts sideways, and more skill and experience are required if the boardsailor is to be able to handle them efficiently in all winds. Their sailing characteristics on a beam and broad reach become progressively more critical as the wind strengthens; the narrow bow dives under the waves, and the increase in directional stability makes it more difficult to alter course quickly. These more unstable round bilge and veed boards are particularly awkward to handle in stronger winds when running, on which point of sailing there is relatively little pressure on the sail, even when the wind is fresh.

With both types of board, the greater the rocker from the centre-board case to the stern the less steady will the board be, especially in a seaway. The term rocker means the curvature of the bottom, the upward curve of the line from bow to stern beneath the hull, as seen from the side. The amount of rocker required aft depends on the breadth of the stern, and should be sufficient to prevent the transom, the vertical or near-vertical stern of the board, from being pressed beneath the water under any sailing conditions.

The bow should curve upwards particularly steeply if the board is to be sailed in medium to high waves, and in surf; the underneath surface of the board should not be immersed very deeply, because it must be possible to sail up the wave and to bear away easily, altering course to leeward when sailing down the wave.

The rocker of boards made of thermoplastic materials, such as polyethylene, can be altered by putting them under load until they take up the desired shape. The surface which has to shrink when the board bends is then heated, the warmth either being provided with sun-ray lamps or, outdoors, by the rays of the sun itself, the heat of which can be concentrated on to a particular area by covering it with a sheet of black plastic. It is essential to bend the board carefully, a little at a time, to avoid the formation of wrinkles in the outer skin. Too high a temperature can also cause the skin to separate from the foam inside, and this results in blisters.

The stiffness of the board, that is, the amount that it will flex, depends on its shape and the material of which it is made. When you bend your knees on the water, a thin beamy board will flex more than a thick narrow board. Polyethylene is the least stiff material; ABS boards (acrylonitrilebutadienestyrene) are somewhat stiffer, while glassfibre reinforced plastics (GRP) boards hardly give at all. In a short steep sea a more flexible board has a slight advantage over a stiff board.

When boards of much the same type but of varying stiffness have been tested, it has been shown that the greater flexibility of a softer board results in slightly greater speed because less of the braking effect of waves is transmitted to the bow.

11

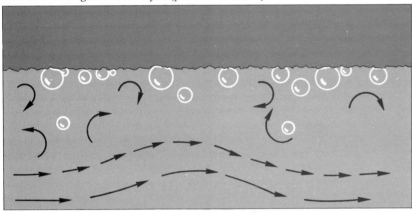

Flow over too rough a wetted surface (porous or scratched).

Flow over too smooth a wetted surface (waxed, polished).

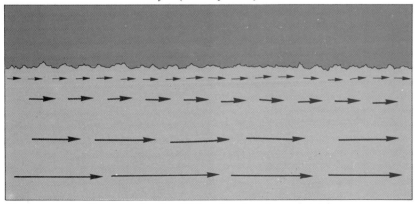

Flow over a correctly prepared surface (400 grade wet-or-dry sandpaper).

PREPARATION OF THE WETTED SURFACE

The owner can do little to alter the shape or stiffness of most boards, and his best way to reduce the total resistance of the board is to reduce frictional resistance to the minimum by improving the wetted surface.

Friction is least when water flows past water, and the aim, therefore is to prepare the surface in such a way that a thin film of water always adheres to it. Consequently the surface must be absolutely free of wax and grease. Although a highly polished surface looks very fast, the water is continuously in contact with the outer layer of the skin (whether gelcoat or polyethylene) and friction is greater than when a layer of water coats the surface.

The correct finish is obtained by rubbing the board down with 400 grade wet-or-dry sandpaper. The surface will then be matt, but speed is more important than appearance when it comes to racing. How well the surface has been prepared can be gauged by pouring water over it, and checking whether a very thin film remains on the skin.

The wetted surface consists not only of the bottom of the hull, but of those parts of the deck over which water flows plus the skeg and the centreboard. The surfaces of skeg and centreboard or daggerboard must be prepared particularly carefully because they are also subject to side force, and friction increases as the square of pressure.

Special and very expensive bottom paints are made for racing boats; they maintain a layer of water on the surface, and thus ensure that water flows past water. In favourable con-

Left: All the wetted surfaces should be rubbed down wtih 400 grade wet-or-dry sandpaper.

Left, below: Flow past rounded and rectangular sterns.

filler, but polyethylene boards present problems because the usual polyester filler does not adhere to polyethylene. However, it is often possible to rub down the edges to make a somewhat sharper angle, and thus improve water flow.

Once the skin has been carefully prepared, it is only sensible to protect it from scratches, undue pressure where it is strapped to a roofrack and other damage.

CENTREBOARD OR DAGGERBOARD AND FIN

The figure on page 14 shows the cross-section or profile shape that is hydro-dynamically correct for the centreboard or daggerboard and the fin. Comparative tests have shown that the leading edge of a streamlined centreboard is particularly important; the sharper the leading edge the greater the tendency for the sailboard to break away to one side, but a more tapered profile has proved to be rather more effective at low speeds. Depending on the sailboard's characteristics and the boardsailor's own skill, it is therefore a question of selecting a centreboard section which can be used when conditions are critical (waves, fresh winds) and which is as close to the section illustrated as possible.

The profile should be thickest slightly further than one-third of the chord length from the leading edge, and should taper to nothing at the trailing edge but, because so sharp a taper would be too easily damaged, the

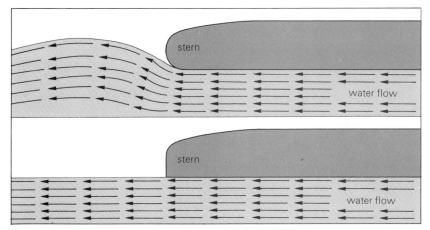

ditions, expenditure on such paint reduces friction resistance by a maximum of about 1%, but the moist underwater surface can be damaged very easily, and must not be rubbed down.

REDUCTION OF RESISTANCE CAUSED BY SHAPE

That part of resistance that is due to the shape of the board can be reduced only in minor ways. Any unevenness on the underside of the board between the fin and the centreboard case must be filled until the surface is absolutely smooth, and then rubbed down.

Frequently the transom is not finished in the most suitable way for racing owing to technical requirements during construction. The transom should not be rounded, but meet the bottom at a clean angle. This can often be achieved by building it up with

13

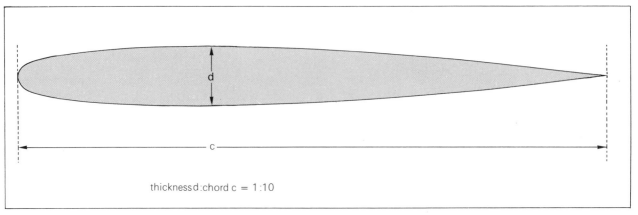

thickness d : chord c = 1:10

Section of centreboard and skeg.

Racing centreboard with a poor section beneath the centreboard case.

trailing edge of a racing board is about 2 mm thick. As a rule of thumb, the ratio of breadth of the profile to the chord is ten to one, as shown in the figure.

The measurement rules of the various classes specify the exact depth measurement. The effectiveness of a centreboard is determined by its profile and its depth, rather than by its area. When sailing close-hauled a centreboard with a chord of about 35 cm and a depth of 40 cm is far inferior to one with a chord of 15 cm and a depth of 93 cm; although the area is the same the latter is far more efficient.

A daggerboard which has to be pulled right out when running and broad reaching in strong winds should have a strap about 2 cm broad and 30 cm long attached to the top; this strap should stick up in a semicircle about 10 cm above the deck so that it can be grasped quickly and the daggerboard hung over one elbow.

The skeg's function is not just to provide directional stability but to

Various centreboard shapes: long and vertical for light breezes, shorter and raked further aft for strong winds.

Reaching with the daggerboard hung over one elbow.

The fin must be firmly fixed to the board.

supplement the centreboard by opposing leeway. The same principles apply for its profile as for the centreboard's, but its size depends on how easily the board will turn. I have made myself a smaller fin to use in waters where winds are light and fluky, so that I can alter course more quickly and make better use of wind shifts. A normal fin can be sawn virtually in half, parallel to the waterline, and the sawn edge sanded down with 400 grade wet-or-dry sandpaper.

The fin should be attached firmly to the board; if it shifts at all eddies will increase. The same is true of the centreboard, but this must also be made to stay firmly in any position, whether lowered, or raised partway or fully, either by sticking a strip of neoprene either side of the dagger-board case or by wrapping sticky tape around the top of a swivelling centre-board. Minor damage to wooden and foam-filled centreboards should be sealed immediately with waterproof glue to prevent further penetration by moisture.

THE STANDING SURFACE

If the area on which the boardsailor stands does not provide a sure enough foothold, a special board wax or a soft ski wax can be rubbed into it. The surface of a new board is often very slippery because some of the separation wax applied to the mould in which it was made remains. This can be removed with a strong detergent, and the surface then rubbed down well with 100 grade sandpaper.

COMPENSATING WEIGHTS

When a racing board weighs less than the minimum permitted by the rules and extra weights have to be added, these are best fitted near the centre-board case. Concentrating weight in the centre of the board discourages excessive see-sawing about the athwartships axis. Only if a board is trimmed too much by the stern or by the bow should the additional weights be fitted further forward or aft respectively.

A hole about 5 cm in diameter is made in the bottom at the selected place, foam is removed to make a hollow that matches the size of the weight which is then pushed inside, covered with a piece of hard foam or cardboard and laminated over. The extra weights can be removed later if the board leaks and becomes heavier as a result of absorbing water.

FOOTSTRAPS

Provided they are allowed by the class rules, footstraps are a great help when sailing in strong winds and in surf. The position at which you stand when using your strong wind sail must be noted exactly. Aft of the centreboard case draw a series of parallel lines about 5 cm apart at right angles to the fore-and-aft axis of the board, numbering them clearly, and a further series of lines either side of the mast foot, angled aft at about 45°. The exact position required for your footstraps is found by checking the numbers of the lines on which you place your feet when sailing in strong winds.

Two slots are made for each strap, using a screwdriver or chisel, and then filled with polyester resin. The ends of the footstraps, which are nylon web-

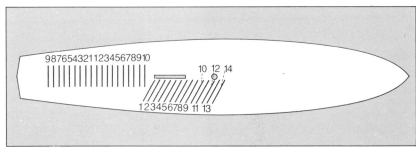

Lines marked on the board like this help you to establish the right position for foot straps.

Straps provide a good foothold in other conditions too.

bing about 25 cm long and 5 cm wide, are pushed well into the slots, leaving enough space for your clenched fist to pass easily beneath them. After the resin has cured, glue strips of neoprene around the bands to keep the straps open permanently as well as to reduce the danger of hurting your feet.

Another but more time-consuming method of attaching footstraps is to laminate four eyes into the board for each strap; nylon webbing is then lashed to them either side. The advantage of this method is that the footstraps can be removed when not required.

The rig

The sail, complete with mast and wishbone boom, is the engine of a sailboard. The shape and the stiffness of the materials of which these parts are made are very largely interdependent.

THE MAST

Round mast sections are specified for all sailboard classes, and we can therefore disregard the question of cross-section shape. The important factors are weight, curvature and strength. As with every other part of a sailboard, the mast should be as light as is consistent with the strength required. Lighter weight means, in particular, that the rig is easier to handle and shift in strong winds.

The strength of a tube increases as the square of its diameter, whereas the increase in strength with the size of the walls and the quality of the material is only linear. Given the same quality of material and comparable walls, a mast with a greater diameter is always stiffer than one with a smaller diameter. The strength of the various materials used for mast-making increases as follows: polyester resin reinforced with glass-fibre, epoxy resin and glassfibre, epoxy and Kevlar, aluminium F 32, epoxy and carbon fibre.

The basic rule is that the stronger the wind the stiffer the mast – to a point where it pays to become more flexible again. For instance, in winds of under Force 2 a more flexible mast is an advantage; the sail will set without creases because there is little tension on the leech. In winds from Force 2 to Force 5, leech tension should be great to prevent the sail from excessive sagging to leeward along the leech. Only when the lateral forces become so great that the sail cannot be held close any longer does a more flexible mast again become necessary. When it bends it pushes the sail to leeward, so opening the leech and allowing the excess of wind to escape by flowing over the sail, which has become considerably flatter.

A great deal depends on the shape of the sail and on the weight and skill of the boardsailor. You will have to decide under what conditions most races will be sailed. Less stiff mass-produced masts can be used in all conditions but, because they bend more easily, they allow the leech to open when the wind is only moderate and, consequently, driving force is reduced when the wind strength is such that the boardsailor could support a greater lateral force.

This mast is not stiff enough.

Here mast and sail match each other well.

17

I have just drawn attention to a very important part of the sail, the leech. The amount of driving force produced depends to a great extent on the tension of the leech which, ideally and in all strengths of wind, should allow the leech to open very slightly. It is the opening and closing of the leech that determines the ratio of driving force to lateral force.

The diameter of some masts is the same almost to the mast tip, and then decreases very suddenly. This sharp reduction is not taken into account when round is cut into the luff of the sail, and in consequence there are almost always creases near the head of the sail; the leech opens more and the vertical camber or fullness of the sail is uneven.

There is no aerodynamic disadvantage to a thick mast with a diameter of over 60 mm, as might be suspected at first glance. Compare it with the mast and sail camber of a catamaran, which often has a very blunt leading edge as a result of rotating the mast a considerable way. I can therefore see no good reason for using a more flexible mast purely to benefit from a reduction in diameter and, consequently, a sharper leading edge.

Glassfibre masts should be reinforced where the loads are the greatest, at the point where the boom is attached and at the foot; most series-produced masts are reinforced at these points.

As to mast length, the logical answer is to make maximum use of the length allowed in the measurement rule because every centimetre of height raises the sail higher, and wind speed increases with height above the water. The sail is much less efficient along the foot, owing to eddies and turbulence caused by waves and the boardsailor's feet.

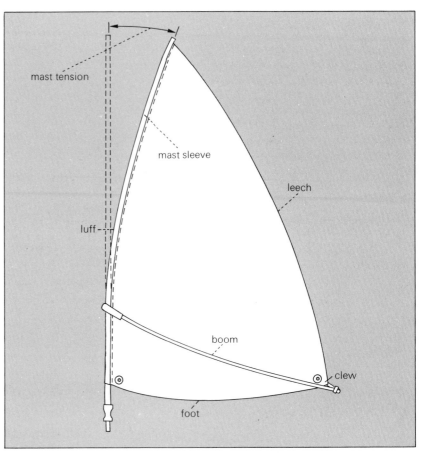

The harder the mast the greater the tension on the leech.

THE MAST FOOT

The mast foot must not jump out of the board during a race, and one with an external mechanical adjustment is ideal. I strongly recommend all boardsailors to increase safety by connecting the rig to the board with a line or piece of shock cord. In stronger winds the board is driven very rapidly away to leeward when parted from the rig, and anybody who has been forced to swim after his board will never again forget this small aid.

The height of the universal joint above the deck affects the tendency of the board to tilt about its fore-and-aft axis in strong winds. The lower the point where the forces generated by the rig are transmitted to the board, the more force is required to make the board capsize. Furthermore the rig's thrust to leeward on the universal joint can be greater without causing the board to tilt over on to the lee rail. Any boardsailor who weighs less than 65 kg, and who is therefore in danger of capsize falling when close-hauled in

Externally adjustable mast foot.

a strong wind, benefits particularly from having a universal joint close above the deck; unfortunately this means reverting to the normal type which cannot be adjusted, because the external mechanical device is usually fitted between the deck and the universal joint.

Hitherto I have found no series-produced board with a satisfactory method of attaching the downhaul to the mast foot. The figures below and overleaf show some solutions:

- A bowline tied above the point where the line emerges from the mast.

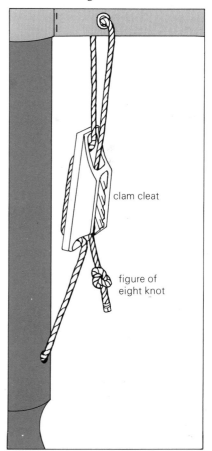

clam cleat

figure of eight knot

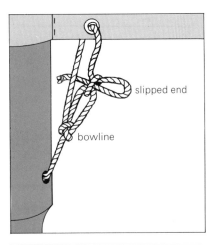

slipped end

bowline

- A clam cleat with the downhaul led through the holes bored for screws.
- A clam cleat screwed or riveted to the mast.
- An additional block fitted to enable tension to be increased (when using a kicking strap, with which the trim of the sail can be altered effectively, an extra line from the mast foot is required).

THE BOOM

The essential points are that the boom should be as stiff and as light as possible, and there are no qualifying factors about the strength of the wind. The most common material used is aluminium tubing about 30 mm in diameter which, when sheathed with one of the many materials available to provide a sure grip, has proved to be very pleasant to hold as well as strength-saving. A section that is slightly more oval in the horizontal plane provides extra resistance to bending without increasing the size so much that it would be awkward to grasp.

The ideal distance between the two halves of the boom varies with the strength of the wind and the weight of the boardsailor. The space between the booms should be as small as possible in moderate and light winds so that the rig can be kept absolutely upright, at right angles to the athwartships axis. A lighter boardsailor, who has to pull the rig slightly to windward when the wind is over Force 3, will find a slightly wider boom more suitable because he can then place his weight further to windward whilst keeping the rig vertical. This holds good for a heavier boardsailor as well, when the wind freshens further, because he can use his weight more effectively when standing further away from the rig. It is not until it is blowing so hard that the rig has to be raked well to windward to reduce the projected sail area that a narrow boom is again required. The size of the waves increases as the wind freshens, and the boardsailor can no longer hang out almost horizontally above the water.

To summarize: A normal boom is a suitable shape, but a wider boom can

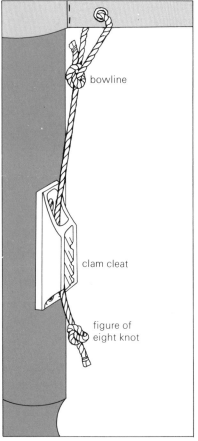

bowline

clam cleat

figure of eight knot

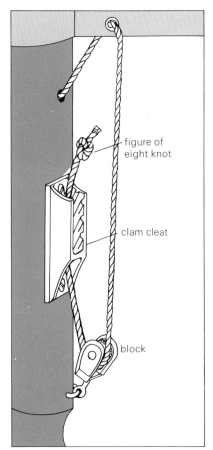

figure of eight knot

clam cleat

block

be advantageous in moderate and strong winds.

The best way to connect the mast to the boom is still with a line. Whether it is simply lashed round the mast or a rolling hitch is made, the line must be led in such a way that the sail can be trimmed freely both vertically and horizontally. I always secure the boom to the mast as tightly as possible to avoid any delay when shifting the rig, and I also find that it makes it easier to react quickly when a gust of wind strikes the sail from leeward.

When a kicking strap is used, the height of the boom can be adjusted according to what the boardsailor finds is best for him. Should the slot in the mast sleeve be too low or too high, another can be made by cutting the cloth with a knife heated in a flame; neither the strength nor the set of the sail will be affected. The higher the boom is attached to the mast the greater the tension on the leech, but foot tension is eased; in the Windsurfer class, where kicking straps are not allowed, this is one way by which leech tension can be adjusted.

The clew outhaul must be particularly easy to adjust because it is the most important control for sail trimming. Quick adjustment is possible if two blocks are shackled or lashed to the after end of the boom, with clam cleats attached either side of the boom where they are within reach. Only when the cringle is so flat that there is excessive friction on the outhaul is a block or carbine hook needed at the clew. No additional fittings are allowed with wooden Windsurfer booms, apart from two closed clam cleats near the places where the boom is gripped; the outhaul is then led through the eyes in the end of each boom (see figure, bottom right, on

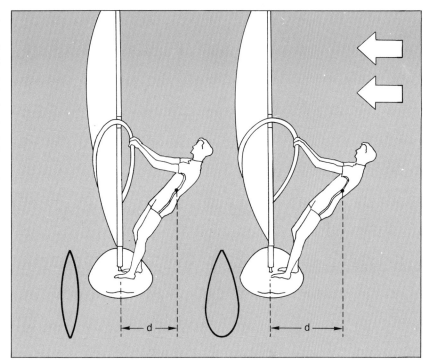

The greater the curvature of the boom, the further to windward the body's centre of gravity (d).

The line attaching the boom to the mast must not affect the set of the sail.

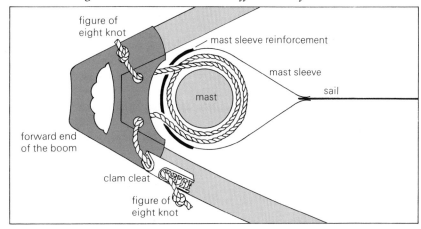

page 22). The two boom ends are bound together loosely with a short length of line to allow them to separate 5–10 cm so that, when pressure on the sail increases, the two ends first pull apart; this increases the tension on the foot.

21

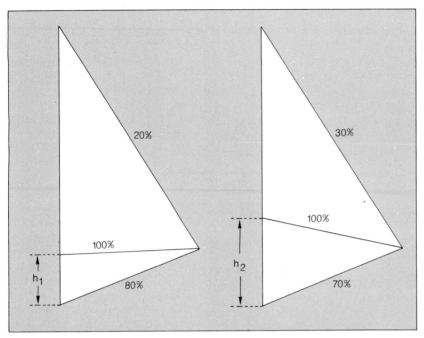

When the boom is attached higher leech tension is increased (h_1 and h_2).

Below: Foot outhaul using two blocks.

Below, right: The outhaul lead for a wooden boom.

It must also be possible to adjust the kicking strap while under way. This leads from the mast foot to a point about 50 cm forward of the after end of the boom, and has a block shackled or attached to it at this end. A second line, which is led through this block and two more at the end of the boom, runs

forward either side of the boom to be made fast in clam cleats within reach of the sail hand.

The uphaul provided with series-produced boards is very suitable, and only requires a piece of shock-cord at the lower end to hold it down, and to keep it out of the water or prevent it from getting in the way when tacking or gybing. The Hawaii-uphaul has a rubber core and is especially good to grasp; it needs no thick knots in it, and can be caught hold of at any point.

Smooth wooden and aluminium booms that are not sheathed where they are grasped make greater demands on strength and, on a long beat, they cause cramp in the forearms and force the boardsailor to change his grip frequently or to support the right with his elbows. Over half this effort is saved if the boom is sheathed with a material that provides a non-slip grip, and all sorts of different sheathings such as neoprene, or self-adhesive suede, leather or buffalo hide are available from specialist retailers. A cheap solution is the self-adhesive textile tape used for tennis and squash rackets, which is not all slippery when slightly damp and weighs very little. Wrap it

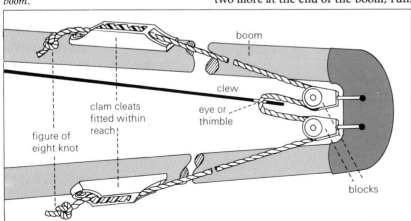

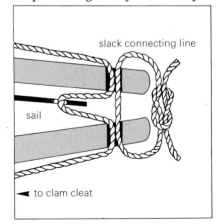

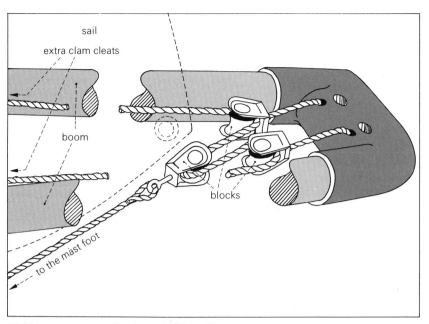

sail

extra clam cleats

boom

blocks

to the mast foot

Kicking strap that can be adjusted while under way.

round the boom, working from a centre point between the hands outwards in either direction, so that the layers overlap in the middle and do not roll back at the edges.

THE SAIL

Theory of sail propulsion – true and apparent wind

The direction from which the wind is blowing can be determined when standing on the bank, looking at the water, but the direction of the wind alters as soon as you get your sailboard moving. The direction and strength of the true wind felt on shore is affected by the wind that results from the movement of the board through the water, and it is the combination of these two winds that decides the strength and direction of the apparent

wind, which will act on the rig. Sailing technique and tactics are therefore based on the apparent wind.

The drawing (page 24) shows how the direction and strength of the true wind are affected by the speed and course of the board, and the factors which make up the apparent wind. On a beat, beam reach and broad reach the apparent wind blows from an angle nearer the bow than the true wind, and the difference in angle can be as much as 30°. It is only when on a broad reach and a run that board speed reduces the speed of the true wind, and this what leads the boardsailor to feel that the wind has eased when he has borne away on to a dead run. When beam reaching and close-hauled, apparent wind speed is greater than that of the true wind; on a dead run the directions of the true wind and the apparent wind coincide.

The effect of sail camber

If we now consider wind flowing over a sail, the streamlines drawn in the figure on page 26 show the direction of flow and the speed of the wind. The closer the lines are spaced the greater the speed.

At the leading edge, the mast, airflow divides to stream over the sail both to windward and to leeward. The air that flows to windward from the luff to the leech travels a shorter distance than the air to leeward, but they rejoin aft of the leech. The consequent differences in velocity of flow to windward and leeward causes pressure to windward to be high, while on the lee side of the sail pressure is low.

Fluid attempts to flow from a high pressure area towards a low pressure area, but because the porosity of sailcloth is extremely low the air does not pass through the sail, and compensation occurs aft of the leech. The resultant force thrusts the sail forward, and is converted into board speed through the mast foot and through the boardsailor's foot.

A sail works most efficiently when its angle of attack to the wind is such that airflow is fully laminar and not turbulent, but it takes experience and a feeling for the wind to find the right angle.

The lower figure on page 25 illustrates some examples of the consequences of varying the angle of attack, and it should be noted that the camber of the sail differs in each case. The degree of fullness or camber has a marked effect on the forces developed by the rig, and these forces are greater when the sail is fuller than when it is flat. Because the angle of attack is less acute with a fuller sail, it is not possible

23

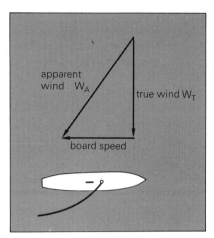

The apparent wind results from the true wind and the wind that arises from board speed.

Airflow over a sail. The streamlines show the speed and direction of the wind.

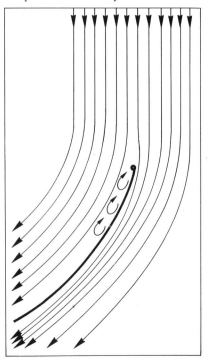

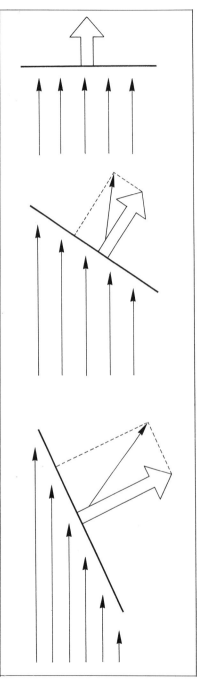

to point so close to the wind, and a compromise therefore has to be made using a ratio of depth of camber to chord length of about 1:10. Thus, given a chord length from mast sleeve to clew of about 250 cm, maximum depth of camber should be about 25 cm. However the depth of camber of such a sail can be varied from roughly 10 to 40 cm to obtain the most effective shape for virtually all angles of attack by adjusting the downhaul, outhaul and kicking strap.

Where should the position where camber is maximum lie?

It is not merely a question of depth of camber, because the curvature of the sail between luff and leech can vary considerably in shape, as shown in the figure on page 26. In practice, the position of maximum depth of camber can be altered only very slightly by adjusting the control lines, and this is a point to bear in mind when evaluating a sail.

The following points have emerged as a result of measurements made in wind tunnels, and I can corroborate them from my own experience:

a) A sail with maximum camber in the centre is slightly superior to sail b) as regards ultimate speed when the wind is constant; however acceleration is slower.

b) Greatest acceleration is provided by a sail with maximum camber in the forward third, and this enables the boardsailor to gather full way more rapidly in gusty winds.

c) A sail with maximum camber in the first half is less effective than the other two, both as regards acceleration and ultimate speed, the only exception being on a run.

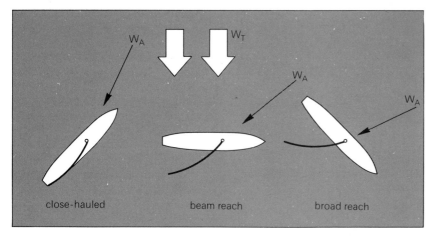

close-hauled   beam reach   broad reach

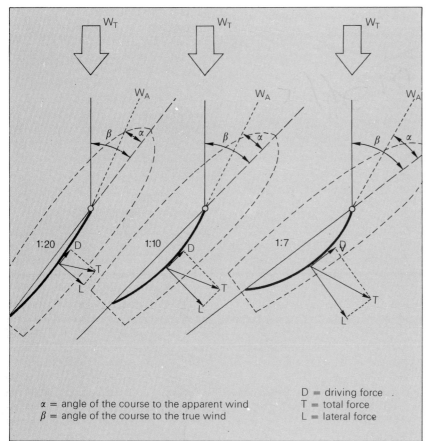

1:20   1:10   1:7

α = angle of the course to the apparent wind
β = angle of the course to the true wind

D = driving force
T = total force
L = lateral force

Sails with maximum camber in the centre are preferred by boardsailors because the superior acceleration provided by the second sail gives only a slight advantage in winds that are particularly variable in strength, but this is countered by lower ultimate speed in more constant winds.

Twist

We discovered why the wind blows in a certain direction and at a certain strength when the board is making way in our discussion on the apparent wind, but another point to consider is that the angle of attack varies at different heights. Although the wind arising from board speed is the same at all heights from the water to the top of the mast, true wind speed increases with height above the surface of the water. In a seaway the wind four metres above the board blows about 25% faster than the wind one metre over the water. For example, a wind that is blowing at about 16 knots at a height of one metre above the board will blow at about 20 knots at the head of the sail and, consequently, when the board is sailing at 10 knots on a beam reach the apparent wind gradually frees to blow from a direction about 5° nearer the stern at the head of the sail; when the board is sailing at the same speed in such a wind on a close-hauled course the difference in angle of attack is only about 2°, but when broad reaching it is about 12°.

Sail camber should therefore vary from foot to head to match the gradual

Left, above: How the sail is trimmed to the apparent wind.

Left: The magnitude of the forces increases with camber.

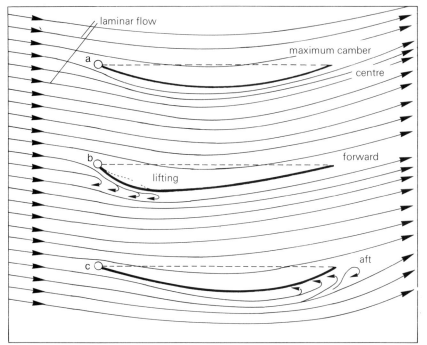

Changing the position of maximum depth of camber affects airflow over the sail.

Within the figure: laminar flow, maximum camber, centre, a, forward, b, lifting, c, aft

freeing of the wind with height above the water. When a sail that is full of wind is viewed from astern it is evident that the upper third of the leech must be open in a wind of this strength.

It is easiest to check airflow by watching the telltales (see page 33).

Cutting sails

Sailboard sails are made of a number of cloths which are seamed together horizontally and run at right angles to the leech. Sailcloth manufacturers weave material in rolls that are 90 cm (metric), one yard (UK) or $28\frac{1}{2}$ in (US) wide and, to save time, most sailmakers use cloths of these widths. However some cut the cloths in half lengthwise, thus obtaining twice as many cloths and seams, for the following reasons:

- When the cloth width is halved, stretch is limited to half the area; furthermore the extra seams not only increase the strength of the sail but prevent excessive stretch and distribute the loads. The sail will not lose shape so quickly.
- When a sail is made fullness is cut into it both horizontally and vertically. The cloths themselves do not curve between the seams, and vertical camber can therefore only be built in at the five seams, each a cloth's width apart. The smoother the vertical camber of a sail, the greater the improvement in airflow, and a more gradual transition can be obtained when half-width cloths are used. It has been proved that the additional seams have no adverse effect on airflow.

The depth of camber required is cut into the sail by shaping the cloths along each side, as in the drawings on the left, while the convex curvature (luff round) cut into the luff allows for mast bend. The degree of curvature of the individual cloths and the amount of luff round are varied to suit the weather conditions in which the sail will be used.

If luff round is generous, the tension on the foot of the sail has to be great to pull out the vertical creases close to the mast. The mast will bend forward and the leech will be taut. A sail with considerable leech tension is especially suitable for moderate to strong winds, provided that it can be set very flat. If the sail is cut with little luff round, the fullness is provided by the curved shape of the individual cloths. When the rig is set up the foot does not have to be pulled really taut to remove creases, and there is also less tension on the leech; the sail is more suitable for light winds because it has a more open leech.

Trimming the sail correctly

Every class association has its measurement rules, and it is obvious that, as far as the sail is concerned, the maximum measurement permitted should be used. However, when breadth at half height is prescribed, it may be possible to increase the area of the sail near the head by not making maximum use of the foot measurement. Extra sail area up high is considerably more effective, because this is where the wind is stronger. The extension of the line of the leech must meet the mast sleeve exactly at the mast tip (see figure top right, page 28) because only then will

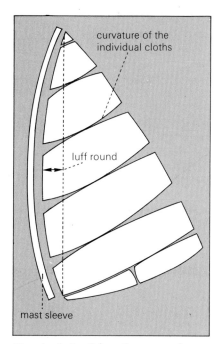

curvature of the
individual cloths

luff round

mast sleeve

How the cloths of the sail are seamed together.

When the sail fills with wind, the long creases at the luff must disappear so that a smooth profile is obtained.

Determining the degree of luff round when making a sail.

tension be exerted on the leech itself, leaving the head of the sail free of creases.

Creases may be caused by too thin a mast tip, in which case its diameter can be increased by wrapping tape around it until the direction of pull on the leech comes at exactly the right point. When the mast is inserted into the sleeve, care must be taken to ensure that the sleeve does not become twisted when the downhaul is pulled taut.

Given a mast of maximum permitted length, the boom can be attached only where there is a gap in the sail, but the curvature of the mast is affected by whether it is attached at the upper or lower end of the gap. The upper part of the mast bends more when the boom is attached higher up and the place where

mast curvature is greatest can be shifted higher or lower by attaching the boom at the top or bottom of the gap.

When the sailmaker decides the line of the luff round, he takes a particular place at the cut-out in the mast sleeve as the point where pressure will be applied by the boom. This point must be found when the board is rigged, because when the boom is attached here the sail will crease least and the profile shape will be smoothest.

Horizontal creases occur in the upper third of the sail when the boom has been attached too high, but if creases appear below the boom, and run to the clew parallel to the foot, the boom is too low. If it is not already large enough the cut-out in the sleeve can be increased in size to eliminate such creases (see page 30).

Luff

In light breezes tauten the luff downhaul until the diagonal creases that run from the mast sleeve towards the clew disappear; there should be no small creases parallel to the mast either. Only in moderate and strong winds should these vertical creases be visible when the sail is empty of wind, especially when a softer mast is being used, because the vertical creases will disappear as soon as the sail fills.

Foot

Foot tension is adjusted with the outhaul and the kicking strap, and should be such that the curvature of the sail is smooth when the wind is blowing at the strength expected, and not so taut that it causes the foot to curl

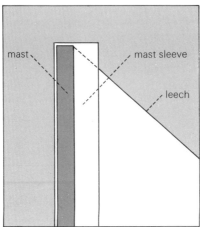

mast
mast sleeve
leech

Above: The extension of the leech must meet the top of the mast.

Left: This luff is too slack.

Below: This leech is closed too much for a beat in light airs.

up to windward. At the point halfway between mast foot and clew, the foot should not sag more than 10 cm to leeward of the direct line between them. Foot tension is adjusted with the outhaul and kicking strap, just as is leech tension; the latter is the more important factor when trimming the sail, and it is therefore sometimes necessary to put up with minor faults in the part of the sail near the foot in order to be able to trim the leech to perfection.

Leech

When the sail or the leech is said to 'open', it means that the horizontal profile of the sail is flat near the leech which, owing to wind pressure, lies to leeward of the direct line between head and clew; if the leech or the sail is said

to be 'closed', the curvature of the sail is continued right to the leech which stands up to windward of this direct line. The great art of sail trimming is to adjust the tension of the leech so that the amount that it opens matches the wind of the moment. When close-hauled, the leech should not be closed by wind pressure; it must lie to leeward of the line from head to clew.

The tension of the leech can be adjusted not only by varying mast curvature, foot tension and the height at which the boom is attached to the mast, but by the kicking strap which could therefore be called the leech tensioner.

It is very difficult to estimate whether the leech is to windward or leeward of the line from head to clew when the rig is set up on shore and full of wind, let alone when standing on the sailboard. I always ask someone to support my rig on land for a short while so that I can convince myself that leech tension is correct by sighting along the line between the clew and the mast tip. When the sail is hardened in gently with the sail hand on a close-hauled course, there should be a slight hesitation along the leech before it closes. This opening and closing of the leech is the point to watch for when trimming the sail correctly for a beat.

For a beam reach and broad reach, sail camber should be increased and the leech closed by easing the clew outhaul slightly and increasing the tension of the kicking strap. The foot will no longer be close to the direct line between clew and mast foot, but the greater fullness of the sail provides considerably more power. Because the angle of the leading edge is less acute, the rig can be held closer than a flatter sail at the same angle of attack could be. Although lateral force is greater driving force is also increased.

In winds of over Force 2, the sail can be made even fuller for the run. It is only in very light airs that it is sensible to project the maximum sail area to the wind by trimming the sail flatter, because airflow is not laminar.

Correcting faults

The set of the sail can be improved as follows:

- Horizontal creases extending up to about 30 cm aft of the mast sleeve – increase downhaul tension.

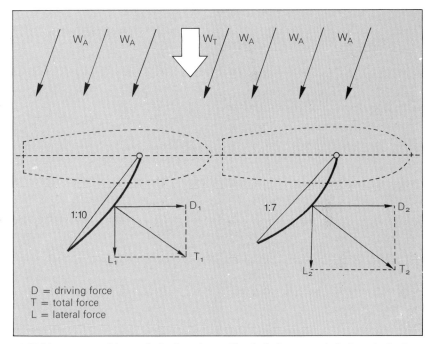

D = driving force
T = total force
L = lateral force

Right: A fuller sail increases driving force on a beam reach and a broad reach.

Hardening the kicking strap closes the leech.

A kicking strap would ease the load on the foot and improve the shape of the sail.

The cloths have stretched along the leech, which is too open.

A flatter leading edge makes handling easier in strong winds.

The shape of this sail cannot be improved, even with battens and a tauter luff.

• Vertical creases parallel to the mast sleeve – ease the downhaul, harden the outhaul.
• The foot rolls back to windward – increase kicking strap tension, ease the clew outhaul, attach the boom higher up the mast.
• Diagonal creases from the top of the mast running to the ends of the battens – ease the clew outhaul, ease the kicking strap, use a stiffer mast.

Faults that can be corrected by the sailmaker:

• Fluttering leech – undo the last 30 cm of the seams near the leech, and restitch them with a slight overlap so that leech length is reduced by about 10–15 mm.
• Leech too flat – in the upper half of the sail, undo each seam for about 50 cm from the leech (but do not unpick the leech seam), and restitch them so that they overlap slightly less and leech length increases by about 10–20 mm.

Faults that cannot be corrected:

• Deep creases along the seams of an old sail – the cloths have stretched, either because the material was poor or because the sail has been overloaded; along the seams, where the material is doubled, the cloths have not lost their shape. Correction is virtually impossible, and such a sail is useful only for training purposes in strong winds.
• Creases running over the entire sail from the mast sleeve to the clew – assuming that these creases cannot be removed by experimenting with and carefully adjusting the trim of the sail, they form because the luff round does not match the character of the mast. If there is too little luff round and no suitable mast can be found, it is a very expensive business to unpick the mast sleeve, remove the cringle and cut in more luff round. In any case the sail will finish up smaller, and no sailmaker will guarantee success.

Trimming the sail for strong winds

As the boardsailor becomes increasingly skilful with practice, he becomes more interested in finding the strongest wind in which he is still able to support the rig and the point at which pressure on the sail exceeds his strength and sailing skills. If you stand on the bank before a race and look at the rough water darkened by strong gusts, at flags fluttering wildly, and at yachts heeling so violently that you become alarmed, it is far from easy to estimate what the wind conditions will be on the course itself, and yet this is what you must do if your are to choose the right centreboard and trim the sail correctly. It is at these times that an

easily adjustable outhaul and kicking strap prove their worth.

As we know already, the ratio of driving force to lateral force depends on the degree of camber of the sail. The more powerful fuller sail with a depth of camber to chord ratio of 1:10 should be maintained as long as you can still support the relatively high lateral force. However, if you cannot close-haul the rig or hold it upright because the wind is too strong, lateral force can be reduced to some extent by flattening the sail. Measurements taken in wind tunnels on wing sails have shown that, in winds above Force 5, a camber of 1:20 produces almost the same driving force but considerably less lateral force. Sail camber can be reduced to as little as 1:30, depending on the stiffness of the mast and how much the cloths are tapered.

You can continue to sail in strong winds by reducing sail area in this way.

There are several other reasons for using a flatter sail in strong winds. One is that when the effect of the increase in board speed on the direction and strength of the true wind causes the apparent wind to blow from a direction that is several degrees closer to the bow, the angle of attack should also be reduced a few degrees, and this is achieved by flattening the sail.

Then again, when close-hauled the aim is to sail at an angle to the wind which gains as much ground to windward as possible. If the boardsailor bears away even only slightly from this ideal course, wind pressure on a fuller sail immediately increases so much that he has to ease out the sail and then luff up again; he will have lost both ground to windward and speed.

Furthermore, the forward third of the sail backs when the wind heads

slightly, and the boardsailor will fall in to windward unless he reacts instantly by pulling the sail over; when the sail is flatter, the angle of attack of the leading edge is more acute, the luff backs later, and he has more time to react.

To summarize: In winds of over Force 5, at the most, a flatter sail is both easier to handle and produces greater driving force; it is therefore certainly more efficient.

A dodge that enables a fuller sail to be carried in strong winds is to shorten the mast; reducing mast length by 5 cm has the same effect as reducing sail area by about 0·1 sq m. Most of the series-produced masts are shorter than the maximum permitted measurement, and are lengthened by adding a mast tip, so it is just a case of stopping up the hole for the mast tip with a champagne

It is usually easier to set a smaller sail in winds of over Force 6, and the board will sail just as fast.

cork and sealing it down securely with sticky tape.

The most spectacular, and also the most effective, method of reducing sail area is to release the downhaul and pull the mast sleeve up almost to the boom. This can only be done when mast and mast foot are securely fastened to each other because, otherwise, the rig could become separated from the board if the sailor fell. When reducing sail in this way, ease the kicking strap tension but pull the clew outhaul as taut as possible.

The individual skill and body weight of the boardsailor often require him to have a strong wind sail as well as a large racing sail. It has been proved again and again that, when the wind is Force 6 or more, the larger sail is not necessarily the faster. A sail cut flat, with either a straight leech and no roach or a concave leech without battens, can still be held upright; the leading edge is still full length, but the area at the leech is reduced considerably, and it is this area which causes the board to luff up willy-nilly when some difficulty arises.

Quite apart from anything else, large sails are severely overloaded in strong winds, and should therefore only be used in an emergency in heavy weather. Racers often have a second, older sail for use when training.

The basic rules of sail trimming hold good for All-round, Medium or Storm sails, namely, keep the camber at about 1 : 10 provided you are able to support the rig; only start to flatten the sail gradually after difficulties start to arise.

The clew board

The set of some series-produced sails can be altered more effectively because they have a metal board at the clew with several holes in it, as opposed to a single eye. Currently a clew board is permitted only in the Windglider class, but the advantages are so great and the cost so small that they will surely soon be accepted in open class racing too. The clew board distributes the great load that is taken here over about 15·25 cm of the clew, rather than at a single point, and so discourages the formation of creases which spread out towards the luff like rays.

The ratio of foot tension to leech tension can also be adjusted more effectively than when a kicking strap alone is used. In lighter winds, lead the clew outhaul through the lowest eye in the clew board so that the leech will not close overmuch when the sail is hardened in. In fresher winds, use the middle or even the upper eye to increase the tension of the leech and so prevent it from sagging to leeward. Not until the board starts to luff up excessively, incessively, indicating that there is too much pressure on the leech, do you lead the outhaul through the lowest eye again.

A more complicated but very effective method is to fit two separate outhaul lines, leading one through an upper eye and the other through the lowest eye so that trim can be corrected while under way. It is advisable to fit a kicking strap as well.

Buying a new sail

The usual reason for buying a new sail is that a new firm, a new cut, or a new material seems to promise a marked increase in speed, but these reasons can be deceptive. The sail can indeed be considered to be the decisive factor

Clew board for adjusting outhaul tension.

when sailboard racing, but there are nevertheless many more reasons why other boardsailors sail faster. It is therefore sensible first to take part in a number of races, and to evaluate your performance as objectively as possible to try to decide whether it is really your sail that is at fault. This may also enable you to compare your sail with those of even more sailmakers before you finally decide whose product to buy.

Sails are made of synthetic fibres, the cloth weight usually being 160 g/sq m (3·7 US, oz). The minimum weight permitted by class associations is 145 g/sq m (3·3 US, oz), but the lighter and therefore the thinner the material the sooner it will lose its shape, even in lighter winds. A cloth weight of 160 g/sq m is certainly adequate for use in light to moderate winds on inland waters, but sailcloth under that weight stretches and loses the camber cut into it in fresher winds. If you will mainly be racing at the coast in stronger winds, a cloth weight of 190 g/sq m (4·4 US, oz) is an advantage in the long term.

Most sailcloth is woven normally, with weft crossing warp. The weft threads, which run across the breadth of the cloth, are more resistant to stretch than the longer warp threads, and the cloths are therefore assembled in such a way that the greatest load on the sail, the load along the leech, is applied parallel to the weft. A very considerable diagonal load also occurs in the area near the clew, and resistance to bias stretch is increased by adding resin filler. The sail will not set so smoothly in light winds because the resin filler makes sailcloth less soft, but the extra stability of the cloth means that the sail will certainly stand up to

more hours of racing without losing shape, and this more than makes up for what is probably its higher cost.

White, the traditional colour for sails, has never really been accepted as the right colour for sailboards – much to the pleasure of photographers. I cannot myself see any good reason for having an all white sail; the area is much too small for any possible minor variations in the strength of the differently coloured cloths to have much effect. The main argument against using a racing sail that is a particularly strikingly colour is that the boardsailor can be identified too easily; if he is over the line at the start, he will be recognized and recalled even when his number cannot be read.

The set of the sail can be affected in certain conditions if very dark and very light sailcloth are combined; black, in particular, is heated more quickly by the sun's rays and then has different stretch characteristics from those of a light cloth which reflects the heat better. This is why I feel that a sail with a black upper half and white lower half is not the most effective for racing; nor are those with similar contrasting colour combinations that extend over larger areas.

A recent idea is to sew a nylon strapping loop to the tack of the sail forward of the mast, and to lead the downhaul, with which the luff is tensioned, through this instead of through a cringle aft of the mast. This avoids pulling down the sailcloth just aft of the mast sleeve, and the sail can therefore set at the right angle of attack. This loop is a definite improvement, especially for light weather sails.

Some sailmakers take the size and weight of the boardsailor into acount when cutting the sail, and in the open

classes the stiffness of the mast has an important effect on the way the sail sets.

Telltales

Very practical aids to trimming the sail correctly are woolly streamers about 15 cm long sewn to the sail. They show whether airflow is laminar or turbulent near the leading and trailing edges. Airflow to leeward as well as to windward is checked by observing the telltales, and small windows are therefore needed if they are to be seen through a dark-coloured cloth.

Theoretically the sail is trimmed perfectly and the ideal course is being sailed when the telltales to windward and leeward are all streaming aft, parallel to the boom, but in practice I find that only the telltales to leeward indicate laminar flow in this way.

If the windward telltales are fluttering particularly wildly, they indicate that the board is being sailed too close to the wind. If the telltales on the lee side of the sail drop to leeward or flutter irregularly hither and thither, either the boardsailor has borne away too far or he has hardened the sail in too much. When the telltales show that airflow differs at various heights, sail twist is excessive and should be corrected by adjusting the kicking strap.

Battens

The purpose of sail battens is to thrust the leech aft and to maintain the camber of the sail at the roach. Battens are made of various materials, in particular, wood, plastics, and wood sheathed with plastics. The important point is that the part nearer the mast should curve more to match the camber of the sail, and this end must therefore be more flexible. Plastic covers fitted over the ends to protect the batten pockets should not be too thick because they can cause small creases to form. Nor need battens fit too tightly in the pockets; that just causes chafe.

CHECKING TRIM ON THE WATER

Having set up the rig on land and corrected the trim of the sail, a further check is needed on the water when under way. Quite often a sail appears to set superlatively well, without a single crease, when there is little wind pressure on it and no load on the boom and yet on the water the board does not point well and makes a good deal of leeway. First check for creasing and for excessive twist near the head; then check the character of the airflow by looking at the telltales. The best way to confirm whether leech tension is correct is to ask someone else to sail the board close-hauled while you follow directly astern, in line with the end of the boom and the mast. When sighting along the leech, the mast should be visible right up to the masthead, just to windward of the leech. Provided that twist is not excessive and that no creases form, the sail will then set smoothly on a beam reach and a run as well.

If the class rules permit alterations to be made to the skeg and centreboard, this is also the time to establish their correct positions and sizes. When sailing straight ahead, it is the position of the centre of lateral resistance about which the board turns that determines the position of the rig and boardsailor. Should the stern be too deeply immersed in light winds when your feet are in

Trying out a new sail for the first time.

the normal position, shift the CLR further forward by reducing the size of the skeg or by moving the centreboard further forward. Replacing a normal swivelling centreboard with a daggerboard of maximum permitted depth will also move the CLR forward because the daggerboard extends absolutely vertically into the water. On the other hand, should there be a tendency to nose dive or bore beneath the waves, the forward part of the top of the centreboard, that is the part inside the centreboard case, can be cut back at an angle to allow the centre-

board to be raked slightly further forward and so shift the CLR further aft. When the centreboard can be swivelled like this to different angles, fine adjustments of trim can be made when under way.

The fresher the wind the more important does directional stability become, and a larger skeg can then be used. Twin skegs are not recommended for racing round triangular courses because the board will not alter course so readily and it takes longer to gybe and tack – optimum directional stability is less important.

COMPARING EQUIPMENT ON THE WATER

A true comparison can be made under way only when conditions and equipment are identical except for the one part being compared. However, the weight, size and skill of the boardsailor himself inevitably affects the result. Assuming that all other factors are equal, first start on a beam reach with the leading board about 5 metres to leeward of the board that is following. Check that the wind is the same for both boards because, often, the leading sailor accelerates sooner as a result of a gust and not because his equipment is different. The best way to make comparisons when close-hauled is for the following board to be about one board length to windward of the leader's wake, and to try to catch up from that position.

The more fluky the wind the longer you should take and the more conscientious you must be for your comparison to be realistic. Leading and following boards should exchange positions frequently, and the boardsailors should check that their feet are positioned so that the sterns of the sailboards are equally deeply immersed.

A final conclusion as to how fast your board sails is nevertheless reached only when taking part in a race series during which you will be engaged in duels with a number of different boards.

MEASUREMENT

Whenever improvements have been made to a sailboard or its speed has been increased by using any of the suggestions described in this chapter, the owner must check that all his gear complies with the measurement rules of the class association. The most important of these are the sail measurements, mast height and centreboard depth.

When the sail is measured it is spread out dry on a flat surface with the battens fitted in the pockets, and the measurement points are then found as indicated in the class rules; the distance that is being measured is extended but not stretched, to avoid the formation of diagonal creasing.

The critical measurement point is the one at the top of the mast sleeve. All the class rules specify that this point is fixed by sighting from the point at which the leech meets the mast sleeve, at right angles to the mast sleeve, to its leading edge. This is the point from which the measurements to the foot and clew are taken, and it is to this point that the clew is folded to find the centre of the leech, which is the measurement point required for half and quarter breadths.

The measurement certificate indicates all the dimensions and the weight of the sailboard, and race officials will probably require you to produce it before more important races. Measurement certificates are issued by the class associations, and exact information is required concerning sail number, board number, measurements and weights. An international certificate is similar, and is often recognized as proof of ownership.

Measuring a sail.

Additional racing equipment

CLOTHING

No boardsailor has become a champion without falling into the water. Racing boardsailors need protective clothing in cold weather to avoid freezing and, sometimes, in order to comply with the requirements of the sailing instructions. Such clothing must not only provide insulation but should also be light and offer the minimum of windage. Unlined neoprene has proved excellent and, although probably not to everbody's taste, the latest tests show that it is still the warmest and pleasantest material in really low temperatures.

A sleeveless long john keeps those parts of the body that are sprayed with water warm. If it is very cold I wear a woolly pullover beneath, and a windproof jacket on top; this gives my shoulders and arms full freedom of movement, but still provides protection from the wind. A close-fitting jacket, which has an adverse effect on blood circulation and on those troublesome forearms, reduces strength noticeably when loads are great.

Synthetic plastics suits with a nylon or terry-type lining are suitable for warmer weather; they feel pleasant and are adequate for air temperatures down to about 10°C (50°F). The thin material deteriorates when exposed to the sun's rays for longer periods, and can also be damaged very easily. When water and air temperatures are very low, I wear an extra waterproof sailing overall on top of my diver's wet suit; although this makes for extra windage, the important factor is not to freeze in such weather conditions.

Gloves and helmets however should be worn only when temperatures are below about 5°C (41°F); because helmets cover the ears, the boardsailor is less sensitive to wind shifts or to increases in its strength, while gloves increase the diameter of his grip and consequently more strength is required to hold the same amount of pressure on the sail.

SHOES

The inventors of boardsailing thought of the sport in terms of swimming clothing and bare feet. The racing boardsailor especially prefers to sail without shoes until the water becomes too cold, but whether it is possible to sail barefoot without injuring your feet will of course depend on the standing surface of the board, how the edges are finished and how much of the centreboard sticks up above the board. It is always faster to sail barefoot; for one thing this saves the weight of shoes which can be as much as 2 kg when wet, for another bare feet offer considerably less resistance to water flow. It is simply a question of getting used to sailing without shoes and every spring I have to reaccustom myself to sailing barefoot again; I find it only takes a few hours before I am fully adjusted, and my sensitivity to speed and the board is then improved.

A simple pair of pumps with soft soles is best if the upper surface of the board is too slippery, or the edges too sharp for barefoot sailing. These only cost about a quarter of the price of

Sailing barefoot saves 1–2 kg in shoe weight and reduces resistance.

those that are made specially for boardsailing, and weigh less but function just as well.

TIMING

A watch is absolutely essential because every race is started literally to the second. Special sailing watches that show five and ten minute periods are available, but an equally good and cheaper alternative is a waterproof diver's watch with a centre second hand that can be set to 0 when the warning signal is made. No great improvement in starting has resulted from trials with digital quartz timers that sound an acoustic signal.

Watch straps with snap clasps sometimes fly open when under load, or if they catch on something, the watch then slips off and overboard; the clasp should be secured with a small piece of sticky tape.

HARNESS

The harness is an important accessory when sailing in moderate and strong winds. It should not be viewed merely as an aid for weaklings but as a sensible and effective accessory that helps the boardsailor to concentrate on tactics and sailing technique, and therefore gives him a greater chance of success.

The idea originated in Hawaii, like so many other sailboard innovations. The Hawaii harness was developed from the trapeze used in sailing boats, but the hook is sited at the chest instead of at the hips. It proved effective from the start, and is now used by most racing boardsailors.

One alternative is the Original-Trapeze, which has the advantage that your back muscles become less tired on longer stretches because you can settle down into it; lowering the point of attachment also improves the leverage of the body.

Whichever harness is used, it is essential that there is an efficient quick release system so that the boardsailor can free himself instantly from the rig if the sail falls on top of him. A device that allows the hook to tilt forward makes it even more certain that the connection between body and boom can be released immediately when under water.

Another method of placing weight to windward is to use bent gloves which transfer the load to the boardsailor's back; considerably less strength is required to hold the boom, and the boardsailor is separated immediately from the rig if he falls.

Other systems are available, but whichever one is used it is still a question of getting used to your harness, and this means spending a considerable time training with it. If you start to get backache, or have weak disc ligaments, a harness with an attachment point lower down near your hips is certainly preferable and can be used for a longer period.

SPARES AND TOOLS

Apart from the sailboard and all its gear, some spares, tools and materials are required between races when competing in a series if repairs are to be made quickly. One of the control lines may be lost overboard when it slips out of a cleat, or a GRP board may be holed, allowing water to penetrate into the interior. A repair kit should consist of:

- Spare rope; large scissors; pocket knife; matches or lighter to melt the ends of the rope where it is cut; sticky tape for trapeze hooks; extra sail numbers (in case two boards have identical numbers and one boardsailor has to alter his); wax; fine and coarse sandpaper; file; screwdriver; pliers; waterproof glue to repair minor damage to wooden centreboards; polyester filler to make good holes in GRP boards; spare battens; spare mast foot.

Tools and gear to take with you.

2 Practising on the water

Sailing technique

It must be said from the start that 80% of driving force, and consequently of board speed, depends on the set of the sail and on the character of the airflow over the sail. The first basic rule, therefore is: **Hold the rig absolutely steady and do not make jerky movements.** This is true even when you are starting from a standstill. After hauling the sail up out of the water, or after having gybed or tacked, you must harden the sail in smoothly and gently with your sail hand until it is full of wind and the board has started to gather way; you will need to use more strength when the wind is stronger, and will also have to make more use of your weight.

BEATING

When starting to make way close-hauled, the sailboard should not at first point too close to the wind. It accelerates very much faster when pointing some 10–15° further off the wind, and you should not luff up to sail hard on the wind until it is moving at a greater speed. In very strong winds your mast hand must pull the rig particularly far over to windward before the sail is hardened in to start to gather way.

It is almost always on the windward legs that a race is won or lost; with an Olympic course (see page 57) the boards will spend about 60% of the time close-hauled, while about 25% is sailed on a reach and 15% on a run. It is not just a question of time, however, because it is also on the beats that there is most opportunity to use tactics and to take advantage of wind shifts or variations in wind strength.

When working to windward, it is not the speed at which the board sails through the water but the distance that is gained over the ground to windward that is important. As every boardsailor soon discovers, the actual speed at which a sailboard moves through the water when close-hauled varies considerably according to how close to the wind he is pointing; the closer he points the slower will the board sail, but he will gain more ground to windward unless he pinches.

The term Vmg, or speed made good to windward, is used frequently to describe the rate at which a sailing boat or sailboard makes ground to windward, as opposed to the speed at which it sails through the water. When beating it is a question of discovering when Vmg is greatest. Some types of sailboard still sail fast when pointing very high, whereas others accelerate markedly when the boardsailor bears away a degree or two. The polar diagram in the figure right shows the speed in knots that a board will make on every point of sailing in a 10 knot wind, and also shows its Vmg when close-hauled but, in practice on the water, it is a question of finding out how high to point by trial and error, and this will depend on the conditions of the moment. It may be a help to know that, given the same board, performance to windward deteriorates as weight increases, as well as when sail camber is excessive or the centreboard too short.

Resistance to forward motion also has a great effect on how close to the wind a board can sail, and a sailboard with a tapering veed bow will point better than one with a blunt bow. The latter planes more easily, but sailboards rarely plane when beating, and those boards that are shaped more like

38

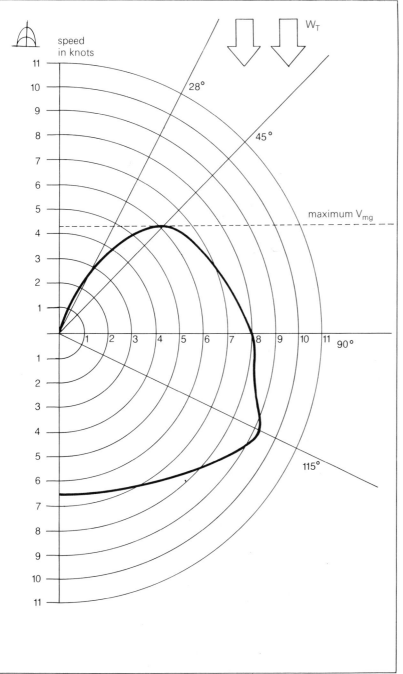

speed
in knots

11
10
9
8
7
6
5
4
3
2
1

28°

45°

W_T

maximum V_{mg}

1 2 3 4 5 6 7 8 9 10 11 90°

1
2
3
4
5
6
7
8
9
10
11

115°

a boat and have a narrow stern are able to sail closer to the wind.

When conditions are right for pointing really high, you should luff up gently and gradually until the board is sailing very close to the wind while still making good speed through the water, but in less favourable conditions pointing high is less important; it then pays to concentrate more on sailing faster, and to bear away slightly instead of keeping really hard on the wind.

Normally the rig is held with the clew immediately above but not to windward of the centreline, but if the sail is very full the clew should be about 10 cm further to leeward. The mast tip should be exactly above the centreline so that the sail is absolutely vertical, at right angles to the wind, until the point comes when the wind is too strong for the boardsailor to project the maximum area of sail to the wind in this way.

The sail can be eased and hardened by the sail hand as much as is necessary to match variations in wind strength, but these actions run counter to the basic rule stated above: hold the rig absolutely motionless so as not to disturb airflow. I have therefore adopted a technique which I find effective, although it is very strength-sapping.

In moderate winds I beat to windward with my arms half bent, stretching or bending them more to match every expected change in wind strength; in this way I use my weight to counter the pressure on the sail, and the rig hardly moves at all. When the wind freshens and my arms are

Polar diagram showing a sailboard's speed on all points of sailing.

39

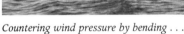
Countering wind pressure by bending . . .   *. . . and stretching the arms.*

experienced boardsailor will recognize the approach of a gust and, just before it strikes, will drop his weight slightly to windward to enable him to make full use of the stronger wind with the sail hardened in.

An approaching gust can be seen on the water, the colour of which changes because the wave structure alters as a result of the stronger wind. The visible difference in colour depends on where the light is – the water becomes darker when the sun is behind you and lighter if you are looking towards it.

Ideally the rig should be raised to the vertical position again at the very moment that the gust eases, so that the maximum area of sail is projected as soon as the boardsailor is able to support it.

AVOIDING CAPSIZE FALLS WHEN BEATING IN A STRONG WIND

The board may start to tilt to leeward when close-hauled in a strong wind for the following reasons:

1. The sail may have been pulled too far over to windward; the rig then transmits too much lift to the mast foot and turns the board over. This tendency can be countered by setting the boom lower; not pulling the sail so far to windward or allowing the leech to open further. If the sail is eased briefly the board will return to its normal trim.

2. Too deep a centreboard; when lateral force increases beyond a certain point your feet can no longer keep the board straight, and it then 'trips' over the centreboard. If the board threatens to do so, and the measures listed above do not help, reduce the centreboard's

already fully extended, I push my hips further towards or away from the sail as they take over the job of countering pressure with weight. I particularly recommend this method when winds are gusty. The object of the exercise is to keep the rig so motionless that airflow is not disturbed, and the boardsailor can check whether he is successful or not by watching the telltales.

Some designs of sailboard have very long vertical surfaces and, in order to reduce leeway, the leeward edge should be immersed slightly when close-hauled, but not to such an extent that it causes water to flow over the deck.

As the wind freshens, move your feet further sideways towards the windward edge until you are finally standing right on the rounded part of the side, in which position the considerably increased lateral force can be transmitted more surely to the board; at this point the back foot's job is to keep the board pointing permanently at the correct angle to the wind.

When the wind freshens beyond a certain point, which depends on the weight of each boardsailor and the area of his sail but occurs in a wind of Force 4 or above, he has to pull the sail over to windward to reduce the area that is projected to the wind, as an alternative to being forced to ease out the sail. An

Capsize fall: the sail, pulled over to windward, lifts the mast foot excessively.

Capsize fall: too long a daggerboard.

efficiency either by raising it or by raking it further aft. You will make rather more leeway but will eliminate the danger of capsize falling, which loses a lot of ground.

BEAM REACHING

Those who boardsail purely for pleasure, rather than racing, can sail best of all on a beam reach – exactly at right angles to the wind as they were taught during the first lesson in a boardsailing school. Nevertheless there are improvements that can be made in sailing technique. Remember that it is the apparent wind that propels the board when it is moving (see page 23). Even a slight alteration in board speed affects both the direction and the strength of the apparent wind and, in consequence, the sail has to be eased out or hardened in immediately if it is to set at the correct angle to the wind. This means in practice that when a sailboard accelerates in a gust the apparent wind heads, shifting slightly nearer the bow, as a result of the increased strength of the wind arising from board speed. If you intend to stay on the same course as before the gust, the sail has to be hardened in slightly; your alternative is not to alter the set of the sail and to bear away a little. In neither case need the movement of the rig disturb airflow because all that is required is a gentle alteration to maintain the angle of the sail to the wind. Conversely, when the gust eases or there is a lull, the apparent wind frees slightly and the sail can be eased out or the board luffed up. Therefore, when sailing a beam reach, either make continuous slight alterations to your course or gently ease and harden the sail to match the apparent wind.

Beam reaching.
The sailboard makes maximum speed on a broad reach.

BROAD REACHING

To a certain extent, the same technique can be used when broad reaching, but the nearer your course is to a run the more should you concentrate on making ground to leeward; in light to moderate winds especially, board speed drops considerably when you bear away on to a run. In a steady wind it is best to sail directly towards your objective, but when wind strength fluctuates, the gusts should be used to sail to leeward of the direct course so that you can sail rather closer to the wind and therefore slightly faster when the wind eases again. You do not need to change the set of the sail, provided that you time your alterations of course to coincide exactly with the changes in wind strength and direction.

In light breezes especially, be careful not to let the transom dip beneath the surface of the water when the board changes speed. If there is any tendency to capsize and the board cannot be made to bear away, raise the centreboard slightly or rake it further aft to shift the centre of lateral resistance nearer the stern; this helps the board to bear away more readily.

On a broad reach and a run the board is far from stable, especially if it has a narrow stern or considerable rocker between the centreboard and the stern. Reducing the area of the centreboard, or its efficiency, helps sometimes; alternatively you can offload the stern by shifting your weight forward until the bow just stays above the waterline. When waves are higher, body weight has to be shifted quickly either further forward or further aft if the board is to be kept trimmed in the best and most stable position.

Capsize fall to windward; shifting weight to the lee side at the appropriate moment helps to avoid this.

To encourage the board to turn, shift weight to the outside edge near the stern.

Frequently the board will alter course automatically when you tilt it slightly sideways. You can practise making it turn whichever way you wish by shifting weight rapidly to one of the outer edges, and if you also move your weight further aft the board will turn more readily still.

RUNNING

You can make the board turn and alter course in this way equally well on a run. When getting under way in a strong following wind, you rake the rig well over to windward and towards the stern as well, and you shift your weight further aft. Bend your mast arm fully, and harden the sail in with a swing with your sail hand, bringing it close over your head. Wind pressure on the sail is greatest before the board starts to gather way, but true wind

speed is reduced by board speed on a run, and pressure on the sail diminishes as the board accelerates. You are then able to adopt the correct and more efficient sailing position, and can concentrate on the trim of the board and the set of the sail. When the board is not on a dead run, it is the pressure on the leech that indicates whether the sail is set correctly or not. If this pressure eases, either the course being sailed has to be altered or the board has to be gybed.

Although the daggerboard may be pulled out when sailing in light airs to reduce the wetted area, the board will become less stable and wobble, which in turn causes airflow to become turbulent. I therefore pull the daggerboard out on a run in lighter winds only when I am not close to other competitors, and am able to concentrate entirely on my course and on

sailing at maximum speed. The sailing characteristics of sailboards vary when the daggerboard is removed in stronger winds, and it depends both on the design of the board and the boardsailor's skill as to whether it is preferable to forgo the rather uncertain and time-consuming business of removing and replacing the daggerboard. If you have no alternative but to pull it out, practise doing this really thoroughly because even a small mistake, say at the lee mark, could make you drop the rig in the water, and this inevitably loses a lot of time.

After having borne away at the weather mark on to a broad reach or a run, pull the daggerboard out at a moment when there is relatively little pressure on the sail, say when just starting to plane down the first wave. Hold the rig momentarily with one hand (the mast hand), and hang the daggerboard over the elbow of your other arm. Above all do not allow the board to luff up; it is not easy to bear away again without the daggerboard and, naturally, time is lost.

The daggerboard should be replaced well before reaching the lee mark so that you are ready to round the buoy perfectly. Thrust it only halfway down at first to avoid risking a last-minute fall, and push it down fully with your foot just before reaching the mark.

SAILING IN WAVES

It is only when the wind is strong and waves are high that the board can be accelerated by surfing on the waves. Just like surfers with their shorter boards, the aim is to try to stay on the steep face of the wave, but sailing on a moving wave, pointing down towards the trough, calls for great sensitivity to speed and motion. The problem is that, if the board is sailing too slowly the wave will slip beneath it and pass on, whereas if the board is sailing too fast the board will dive into the trough and probably bore into the back of the wave ahead.

The art is to keep on the right course in relation to the direction in which the wave is travelling and stay sailing down its face for as long as possible. When the wind is steady the wave will certainly travel to leeward faster than the board will sail if the boardsailor is on a dead run, with the rig held athwartships ahead of him, and makes no attempt to plane. It is then a question of luffing up to a broad reach to accelerate and plane on the wave. When you find a suitable wave, bear away on its face and shift weight forward, easing out the sail and hardening it sharply once or twice to

(e) Gradually harden the sail.

increase your speed further. Pumping by trimming the sail rapidly in this way is permitted only in such circumstances because the racing rules specify that pumping may be used only to promote or initiate surfing or planing, and not to maintain either state.

As soon as the board starts to surf on the wave, its speed increases and the sail therefore has to be hardened. If the bow appears likely to dive into the wave ahead, luff up and sail diagonally along the wave, but if the wave starts to catch up, bear away slightly more.

It takes practice and concentration to sail a snaky course like this, but speed increases considerably and it is extremely exciting – provided you are sufficiently skilful.

Using the wash of motor boats

On inland waters, waves are relatively small and unsuitable for surfing, but a large motor boat will often raise waves which can be made use of, and you will benefit from a considerable increase in speed if you can stay on the wave. In

(d) Sail hand crosses over.

the European championships in La Mange, Spain in 1979 I got a good start and was then able to use the stern wave of a spectator motor boat while making a long tack. My speed increased so much that I ignored wind shifts entirely, and did not go about until I could fetch the weather mark on port tack; although the wind then headed me I led the whole fleet at the end of the windward leg.

Such opportunities do not occur very often, but I feel that it is nevertheless worth practising making use of waves in this way. It is not always easy to stay on what is generally a short steep wave, and the wind direction and strength must be right, but just attempting to maintain the right speed and the correct course gives you the feel of surfing, and makes it easier to learn how to surf on wind-raised waves.

(c) Mast hand grasps the mast and pulls it forward.

(b) Boom end down towards the water; harden the sail slowly.

Racing tack: (a) Close-hauled.

Manoeuvring the board

TACKING

The beginner is taught how to put a sailboard about in the very first lesson, but this basic method can be improved on and the figures above show the complete sequence of a fast racing tack.

Start by raking the mast aft until the clew is just above the stern of the board, and harden the sail in gradually, keeping it full of wind. Grasp the mast beneath the boom with your mast hand and step round the mast. It is not until the board is within about 10° of the new course that your sail hand releases the boom, your mast hand rakes the rig forward, your sail hand reaches over to grasp the other side of the boom, and you then quickly pull the boom in with your new sail hand until the sail fills with wind, gently hardening it to the correct close-hauled position.

The important point is to complete the critical phase, when there is no wind pressure on the sail, as rapidly as possible; your actions must be quick and certain when you grasp the boom on the opposite side and harden in to fill the sail. The most common faults, which I see being made repeatedly even by experienced racers, are:

- Changing the sail from one side to the other too soon, before the board has started to make way on the new tack. Take a little longer to enable you to bear away further.
- Changing grip too often owing to insufficient practice on the sequence of movements. Time is wasted and movements are less assured, especially when the wind is strong.
- While stepping round the mast and shifting hands over-frequently there is no wind in the sail for too long a period, the board slows, loses way and may even be driven back stern first.
- Pulling the sail back too far to windward of the centreline, to initiate the tack. The sail held back against the wind brakes board speed. When the wind is light all movements must be particularly gentle and gradual, and the board will then be able to shoot about one length dead into the wind, so gaining extra ground to windward.

Board speed is braked if the boom is pulled back too far to windward.

In strong winds the board can be encouraged to turn by standing aft of the centreboard case with the rig, and forcing the bow up towards the wind. After grasping the boom with the new mast hand, allow the rig to drop slightly to windward before taking hold of the boom with the new sail hand, so that you are able to use rather more weight to counter the higher initial forces on the sail.

When you have to go about in higher waves, start by luffing up just when the bow starts to sail down a wave so that the critical unstable stage occurs right in the trough where the board is least disturbed by turbulence. The sail is hardened in just before the next crest, and the wind will not then act at full strength on the sail until after the board has started to make way.

When the wind is strong a particularly good moment to tack is when a gust has just eased because the sailboard is still moving fast, and can shoot up towards a wind that has become rather lighter. Furthermore there is then less danger of falling to windward if the luff backs when the sail is hardened in.

GYBING

Theoretically the board only has to be gybed twice during a race round an Olympic triangular course, once at the reaching mark and once at the lee mark, but a boardsailor who makes full use of wind shifts and gusts will often gybe nearly as frequently as he tacks.

Racing gybe: Beam reaching.

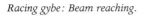

Weight on the outer edge, rig raked to one side.

Do not shift the rig to the other side until the board has swung 30°, round on to the new course.

When carrying out a racing gybe that involves a considerable alteration of course, the sail should remain considerably longer on the original tack than is taught initially whatever the strength of the wind. At the very earliest, the sail hand does not release the boom and grasp the mast until the board has swung about 20° beyond a dead run, and it then pulls the rig over to the opposite side while the end of the boom swings round over the bow. The new sail hand then catches the boom and holds the rig in the desired position, while the forward hand moves from mast to boom. In moderate and strong winds, the board can be encouraged to turn by putting weight on the side of the board that will be on the outside of the curve sailed while gybing, that is, the side opposite to the direction in which the board is to turn.

The best time to gybe is when sailing at a good speed, either down a wave or towards the end of a gust, because pressure on the sail is then least and it will be easier to harden in the sail on the opposite gybe.

When the board is gybed on a run, and there is little alteration of course, the stage when the sail is being swung round must still be accomplished very quickly so that the time when the sailboard is not being driven forward is kept as short as possible. Common faults when gybing are:

- The sail hand lets go of the boom too soon. In winds over Force 2 the boom will not swing over to the other side, and time is wasted before the sail again produces maximum driving force.
- The board turns the wrong way because weight has been put on the inside edge. The rig is raked to one side to turn the board in one direction, but it turns the opposite way, taking up a good deal of space on the water and wasting a lot of time.
- Clew not close enough to the water when the sail is swung round. This reduces the turning force of the rig, the gybe will be slow and, again, will take up a lot of water.

I regularly practise gybing afresh at the start of every season, and have improved my technique. During a race there must be no risk involved, and every gybe should be perfect. The

Luff up to the correct course.

Grasp the mast with the mast hand.

Swing the rig round with the end of the boom just above the water.

ideal is to practise on a slalom course with at least six buoys laid in a line, about six to ten metres apart; to start with, sail the course slowly and concentrate on tacking and gybing absolutely correctly; only later should you speed up your actions gradually as you become more sure. It is above all in light to moderate winds that perfect technique and accurate turns will pay off, but in strong winds too you must be especially sure of all your movements because a fall immediately results in a considerable loss of distance. I have seen boardsailors fall at the reaching mark, touching the buoy as they do so, and they have then had to let as much as a third of the fleet pass by before starting off in pursuit.

It is not just a question of being able to go about and gybe under full control, turning as fast as possible while gaining ground to windward or to leeward respectively; you also need to practise making sudden and abrupt turns so that you can react instantly in case of emergency. Quite frequently you do not notice that a competitor is approaching on starboard tack until the last moment, and there is then generally no time to go about carefully.

To luff sharply, pull the boom end to windward and thrust it down, simultaneously raking the mast slightly to leeward so that you lose way. Use a stop gybe to bear away when winds are no more than moderate; the sail hand releases the boom and pulls it back on the opposite side, with the clew just above the surface of the water. Turning the board in this way reduces speed abruptly and, in stronger winds, shifting weight aft and to the side of the board that is on the outside of the curve makes the turn even tighter.

To luff up rapidly and lose way quickly, pull the boom over to windward and dip the end in the water.

SAILING STERN FIRST, AND DRIFTING DOWN TO LEEWARD

Sometimes, during the last few minutes before the starting signal is made, the boardsailor needs to stay close to his chosen starting position, instead of drifting further down to leeward. The board is often so hemmed in by other competitors that there is too little room to tack twice to gain ground to windward, and it is then that experts use the falling leaf technique. This involves sailing backwards and forwards in curves, in rather the same way as leaves fall from a tree. Instead of turning the bow through the wind, the board is sailed back and forth, alternately bow first and stern first, and covers about 5–15 metres in each direction, depending on how much room there is on the water.

When sailing stern first, the stern must be prevented from immmediately luffing up into the wind; the centre of

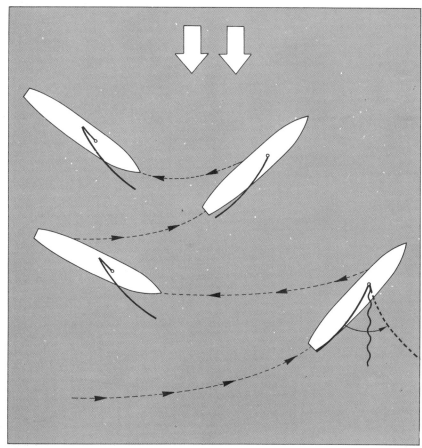

The falling leaf technique. Beating forwards and backwards without tacking.

effort of the sail has to be kept above the centre of lateral resistance. This is achieved when the mast tip is roughly over the transom. Shifting weight to the windward edge also turns the stern away from the wind slightly. The boom end will be very high above the water and should be roughly over the centreline, and it can be pulled further to windward to make the board bear away without increasing speed excessively. Make sure that there is enough room to leeward for the boom

to swing round when changing to sail in the opposite direction.

Practise in open water first. It is very noticeable that, when sailing backwards, the board can be steered more effectively by tilting it to one side than by altering the position of the centre of effort. This is mainly because what are now the leading edges of the centreboard and skeg taper almost to nothing, and a strong tendency to turn results immediately from any change in the angle of attack. Furthermore,

when there is even only a small deviation from the direction in which the sail is thrusting the board through the water, the effective area of the fin becomes greater, and the board has a more marked tendency to alter course to windward.

Once you can steer the sailboard straight stern first, look for a buoy or marker near which you will stay while practising the falling leaf technique. Start about a metre to leeward of the buoy, and let the board drift a few metres further to leeward in response to wind and waves; then work back to it sailing alternately stern first and bow first, covering no more than about five metres in either direction.

A board with its sail shaking will drift to leeward most slowly when it is exactly at right angles to the wind. When it is turned slightly towards the wind, rather smaller areas of the side, the centreboard and the skeg are presented to oppose leeway, and the board will drift downwind faster. Therefore, when a board is not making way, the speed of drift to leeward can be controlled by altering its angle to the wind and, as a result of practice and of timing the rate of drift with a watch, the boardsailor can estimate far more accurately how long it will take him to drift down to a certain position.

This sort of practice proves its worth when it comes to manoeuvring in a congested fleet a few minutes before the start of a race, when boards are lying only a few centimetres apart and must not come into contact. The situation becomes critical if the sail fills with wind and the board is driven forward unintentionally, because you may then either be unable to keep clear of motionless competitors ahead, or be forced to cross the line before the starting signal, and the consequence could be a protest against you made by another competitor or by the race officers.

This can be avoided if you practise losing way completely without altering course; the method is the same as when starting to sail stern first, but you rake the mast tip further to windward and harden the sail in only until the board has ceased to make way.

Sailing with a harness

When you are using a harness the distance between your body and the boom should also be as great as possible. The Hawaii harness lines are therefore attached to the booms either side in such a way that the boardsailor can grasp the boom easily when hanging right back in the harness. The lines and the nylon straps provided with the harness are usually too short. A line should be attached to each boom with the ends as far apart as possible, because the greater the distance between the two attachment points the lesser the boom bend when under load. It can even be made fast aft of the cleat with a rolling hitch and to the forward end of the boom with a bowline, and leave the area where your hands grasp the boom completely clear. When the hook is high, the taut lines may occasionally get slightly in the way of your upper arms, but I do not find this particularly troublesome because real tension comes either only on the line or only on the upper arms.

Sailing close-hauled, stern first.

The nylon straps are each passed twice round the boom, and the lines are either attached to the eyes with bowlines, or are led through the eyes and a figure of eight knot made in each end. Check that the long end of the line leads from below into the loop of the figure of eight, and also that the short end protrudes slightly from the knot.

The position of the ends of the line in the area that is grasped depends largely on the position of the centre of effort. When using a harness, the after hand must exert some pressure on the boom to ensure that the sail can be eased out

if there is an unexpected gust because, if wind pressure acts too far forward, even a slight increase in wind strength can lead to a catapult fall; instantly, the sail is hardened in automatically and will then exert even more force on the boardsailor.

This is another reason for attaching the Hawaii harness lines at positions that are as far apart as possible; the point at which pressure is applied can then be varied while under way without having to adjust the harness line.

When the wind is strong and waves are high, and the rig cannot be held sufficiently far to windward by hanging in the harness because your body would be too close to the water, shorten the loop that sags down by slinging it once or twice around the boom. Pressure can then be applied at the correct point by shifting this smaller loop sideways with the harness hook.

Some Hawaiians sail with the hook opening upwards when the boom is attached very high; they claim that this makes it easier to hook themselves on, and that they can release themselves more quickly if there is a danger of a catapult fall, but it must be noted that the line is rigged only about 10 cm away from the boom where it hangs immediately above the open hook.

I use a harness mainly in winds of over Force 4 on the windward legs of a triangular course in order to conserve my strength for the reaches and the run. It is rarely possible to use the harness when the wind is free and, in practice, when sailing off the wind and when hardening and easing the rig while surfing on the waves, there is a greater risk of becoming hooked on by mistake, and consequently of being pulled off balance. To avoid this I sling the loop of the harness line round the boom once or twice to keep it out of reach of the hook, and I also hold the free end of the line with my thumb so that nothing untoward can happen.

I have got into the habit of taking the harness with me even when the possibility of the wind exceeding Force 4 is no more than slight, and I then wrap a piece of sticky tape around the hook to avoid becoming hooked on unintentionally; the tape can be ripped off easily if the wind does freshen. It may well be that, soon, this idea will be adapted by sewing a strip of nylon tape

to the plate and fastening it over the hook opening with velcro.

The sail sets more quietly and closer to the wind when the boardsailor hangs out in a harness, especially in a strong but steady wind. Even though the board would sail at maximum speed only when his arms were fully extended and his weight far to windward, the harness can mean greater speed in the long term. However, if you are duelling with another board, when losing one metre could immediately cause you to fall into your opponent's wind shadow, I strongly advise you to unhook yourself because, when in direct contact with the sail, you will be able to sail at top speed while pointing as high as possible. I also consider that this is necessary if you slightly misjudge the moment to tack for the weather mark, and have to sail the last 50 metres particularly carefully, pointing very close to the wind.

Building up your strength on the water

A boardsailor still needs a considerable amount of strength, even if he uses a harness, and training to increase your strength and fitness undoubtedly pays off when it comes to handling the rig when tacking, gybing and altering course, and when sailing long reaches in strong winds.

One way to become fitter and to increase your reserves of strength is, of course, to sail in strong winds without a harness for a very long time until your forearms become thickened and pains shoot through the muscles. This was the method I adopted in the early years, and found after a week of training that I could support the rig considerably longer in winds of over

Seal the opening of the harness hook with sticky tape when the wind is light.

Force 4. However I also found that my reserves of strength were considerably lower if I had to exert maximum effort immediately, without having been able to increase the load gradually beforehand. Then I tried sailing really hard for about 15 minutes, a period which caused me no pain, followed by a rest of about the same length of time. When I set off again I discovered that I could sail about 30–50% longer than when I had not paused.

The reason is that, after initial strenuous exercise, there is an inadequate supply of blood to the forearms and, when muscular tension is released, the blood vessels dilate and an improved circulation results in increased energy, which is adequate to supply the energy requirement of the muscles when under load. This is why muscles are warmed up before a longer period of continuous work.

Training conditions with day-long winds of over Force 4 seldom occur, and other methods therefore have to be used as well. One is to set an oversize sail, designed for use in very light airs, when there is a Force 3 wind. Given an area of 7–9 sq m, a very stiff mast is needed to provide sufficiently great lateral force in so light a breeze. If the luff of the sail is long enough, two normal tapering masts can be used, one pushed inside the other, and this not only provides the length needed but also considerably increases mast stiffness. A further advantage is that, because of its greater weight, more strength is required to raise the rig from the water, to harden the sail, and to counterbalance the forces on the rig and, consequently, the muscles used for these purposes are more heavily stressed. Regular training strengthens the calf and back muscles in parti-cular, and when you return to the smaller and lighter racing rig you find suddenly that it can be handled very much more easily.

You can handicap yourself in other ways without using a larger sail. If you fill the mast about two-thirds full of water before sailing a slalom course and practising rounding buoys in a wind of over Force 3, you will need to use considerably more strength to handle the rig, and will learn to make better use of momentum. Alternatively you can increase the weight of your trunk by putting on several thick woolly pullovers, plus a buoyancy aid on top; soaking the pullovers with water will greatly increase your weight. Intensive training of this sort should be carried out systematically over a period of one or two weeks, during which you increase the loads gradually, but you must allow a day or two afterwards to reaccustom yourself to the lighter racing rig, to the reduction in driving force with the smaller sail, and to the decrease in your body weight.

The results of such training do not become apparent before about five days, because the body can only adjust slowly to demands on strength.

Determining the tacking angle

It is when approaching the windward mark at the end of the very first beat of the very first race that a novice discovers he is unable to measure angles and distances by eye, and that he does not have the experience to judge when the right moment has come to tack for the mark. This is important because every unnecessary metre that the board overstands the mark by staying too long on this tack is distance lost and equally, if he goes about too soon, he will have to put in two extra tacks, and will again lose distance.

Part of your race training programme should therefore be to practise going about to fetch the mark on the opposite tack. First a little theory based on sailing boats: just like other sailing craft, a sailboard can sail close-hauled at an angle of 45° to the wind, and the sum of the angle of two tacks is therefore 90°.

This figure of 90° gives a rough indication of the course that will be sailed after the board has tacked. When a board is close-hauled on one tack and being sailed correctly, high on the wind, and an objective lies at right angles to the centreline, it should be possible to sail straight to that objective on the opposite tack after going about, always assuming that the wind does not shift and that the current or tidal stream is negligible.

The actual angle varies somewhat from 90° according to the type of sailboard. The Windsurfer, for example, does not point as close to the wind as some of the displacement type boards that compete in the open class. This is due partly to the fact that a longer centreboard is permitted in the open class, and partly to the differences in the hulls' resistance to forward motion, the stiffness of the masts and the lengths of the leading edges of the sails.

Blanketing the boardsailor to leeward to prevent him from overtaking.

The boardsailor has to establish the angle through which his sailboard tacks so that he knows where he will be heading after he has gone about and, when sailing alone, it is best to do this by making longish tacks. Before going about you estimate where the board will be heading on the opposite tack; you then go about and, after sailing high on the wind for 50–100 metres you will soon discover whether your estimate was correct or not. It is obviously essential that the wind direction should be relatively steady, and an onshore wind on a larger lake or at the coast is usually the most satisfactory. When sailing in conditions where Vmg is greater if the board is sailed slightly off the wind, the angle through which the board tacks will obviously be rather greater than when sailing in ideal conditions.

Open class sailboards are permitted to use two different centreboards, and the tacking angle for both must be established. When racing in a series, it is not always easy to adjust immediately to the new tacking angle after having changed centreboards, and it is advisable to base your decision when to tack on the more obtuse of the two angles, especially when you have changed to a shorter centreboard.

Wind shadow

One way to prevent a following board from catching you up on the beat, or to slow down a board ahead on the run, is to keep him in your wind shadow, the effective area of which extends about thirty metres to leeward. When your board is close-hauled, the direction in which this turbulent zone lies is not at right angles to leeward of the board, but dead downwind of the apparent wind.

It is rather easier to establish the whereabouts of the wind shadow when sailing in a boat with a burgee at the masthead, and you can then keep an opponent firmly within it, or avoid being blanketed by another boat. The figure below shows the size and direction of the shadow when a board is on a run, on a beam reach and on the wind.

It is good practice to try to keep another board in your wind shadow on various points of sailing when you are sailing with a friend; exchanging your positions will improve your ability to estimate the extent of the wind shadow and the angle at which it lies.

Beware of larger sailing boats with considerably greater wind shadows while you are racing. You will be caught in one when the boat's burgee, which indicates the direction of the apparent wind, is pointing directly towards you.

Where the wind shadow lies on a run, a beam reach and when close-hauled.

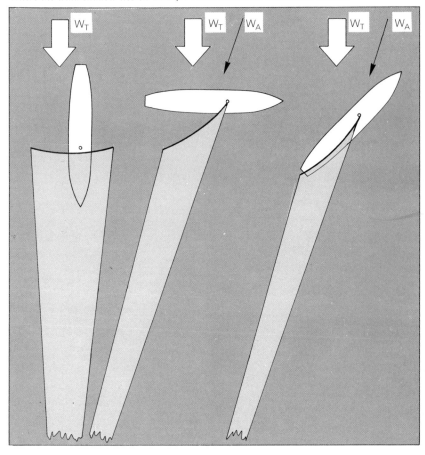

Safe leeward position

The wind near a close-hauled sailboard is not only affected in the wedge-shaped area of the wind shadow but elsewhere. The illustration (right) shows how the wind is deflected by sails, and it can be seen clearly that the wind to weather of the board is deflected to head slightly, blowing from rather nearer the bow, whereas to leeward the wind frees a few degrees.

When the courses of two close-hauled boards cross during a race, and one boardsailor can tack into this area where the wind frees a little, he will then be in the safe leeward position and can either luff up or ease his sail slightly to get ahead of his component. Because the leeward board also has right of way and can luff the board to windward, there will be no unfortunate consequences, but it is important not to go about too close to the windward board, which may luff up quickly to try to catch the other in his wind shadow.

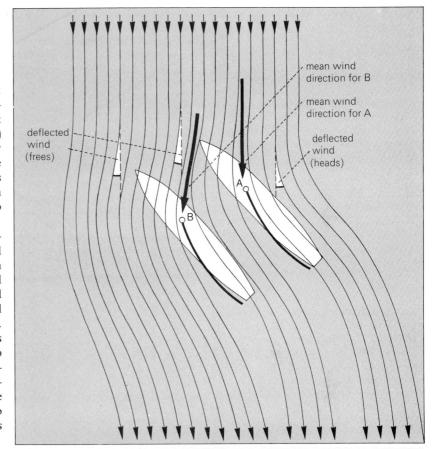

mean wind direction for B

mean wind direction for A

deflected wind (frees)

deflected wind (heads)

A

B

Above right: The safe leeward position; how airflow is deflected by a sail full of wind.

Right: F 113 has broken clear of the wind shadow of the boards to weather, and is in the safe leeward position.

One method of training

When you sail alone, your sensitivity to speed on all points of sailing improves the most. I have noticed again and again that newcomers to racing point well when sailing in company with other boards, but do not always sail the best close-hauled course when they are alone; they generally tend to sail slightly off the wind, because the boards are then moving faster through the water. It is absolutely essential, however, to be able to sail the optimum course when nobody is nearby to guide you, and it is best to practise sailing close-hauled alone to sharpen your sensitivity so that you recognize when you are pointing well at the same time as maintaining good board speed. You have to learn to become aware subconsciously when the board is no longer sailing the optimum course; there are so many other things to concentrate on during a race that something has to be done automatically without causing a reduction in board speed.

You can check just how well you can sail subconsciously when close-hauled if a friend with the same type of sailboard follows slightly astern of you and to windward, as described in the section on comparing equipment (see page 35). He should sail as carefully as possible, checking the position of his rig, his course and the set of the sail while, ahead of him, you try to sail fast and point well without looking at either your rig or at his. When you use this method of training the following boardsailor can also draw your attention to any errors you make, such as excessive movement of the rig, that you are sailing off the wind or that your leech is too open. You will find that you gradually acquire the sensitivity to make the fine adjustments that are required when the wind shifts and, once you can do so automatically instead of consciously, not only will you sail faster but you will have more time to consider your tactics and the actions of your opponents.

Training to improve board speed on a beam reach.

3 Racing

The triangular course

A sailboard race, like a normal sailing boat race, is usually sailed round a triangular course with buoys marking the end of each leg. The first leg runs from a starting line towards the wind to provide a beat, and is followed by two reaching legs, a second beat, a run and a final beat to the finish, as in the figures on the right. One alternative, when a race course is laid in confined waters, is to sail two more reaching legs before the final beat.

The race officers inform the competitors of the direction in which they must sail round this triangle; a red flag is often broken out to indicate that all marks must be left to port, or a green flag when they are to be left to starboard. It is the place in which the board finishes that counts, not the distance nor the time interval between two finishers.

Above, right: An Olympic course with the start at the lee mark and the finish at the weather mark. Compare this with an Olympic course with a separate start and finish (below).

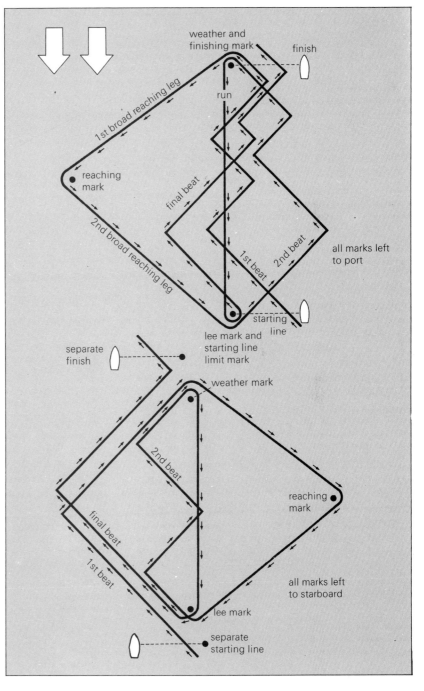

weather and
finishing mark

finish

1st broad reaching leg

reaching
mark

run

final beat

2nd broad reaching leg

1st beat

2nd beat

all marks left
to port

lee mark and
starting line
limit mark

starting
line

separate
finish

weather mark

2nd beat

reaching
mark

final beat

1st beat

lee mark

all marks left
to starboard

separate
starting line

Points systems

In Britain, the RYA short series scoring system may be used, and the first board to finish a race receives $\frac{3}{4}$ point, the second 2 and all other finishers the same number of points as their finishing places. The Olympic points system, which is widely used in many countries including Britain, gives an advantage to the first six finishers: 1st 0 points, 2nd 3 points, 3rd 5·7 points, 4th 8 points, 5th 10 points, 6th 11·7 points. From 7th place onwards points are added to the finishing place, e.g. 9th 15 points.

The Olympic scoring system is based on a series of up to seven races; the worst result can usually be discarded and the series winner is the man with the lowest total score. Sometimes when seven races are sailed the two worst scores may be discarded, but when less than five races are sailed the one in which the highest number of points has been scored usually has to be counted. The sailing instructions indicate how the winner is decided if two boards finish with the same total; for example it may be the board with the most first places, the one that finished ahead in the last race or the one that finished ahead of the other most frequently. Occasionally the discarded result has to be included in the total to break the tie.

Differences in the number of points awarded could occur if a competitor did not start in a race, or started but did not finish, and the number of boards competing therefore has to be established before the start of the series. Sometimes each board has to inform the committee vessel of his presence at the start so that the number of boards ranking as starters is known.

In order to win the series, a board must be well placed in the individual races, and that means sailing as fast as possible and trying to gain places by taking some tactical risks. Points totals and finishing places become more critical and tension increases towards the end of a series, and it may well be that all your attention has to be concentrated on a single opponent who must not be allowed to finish ahead of you because of the points situation. This can be explained most easily by giving an example (based on Olympic points).

Given that a total of six races will be sailed and one discard is allowed, strategy during the last race must be based on the points situation, and it is assumed that the points total of all other opponents is too high for you to have to worry about them. You can win the series either by winning the last race (total 25·4 points), or by finishing 2nd, 3rd or 4th (totals 28·4, 31·1, 33·4) with Opponent I at least one place and Opponent II two places behind you. If you finish 5th or worse but ahead of both, Opponent I will win the series with a total of 33·7, having discarded the result of the last race.

Given seven races with two discards the final result is even more open and you appear to have a good chance because you can discard your 6th and 10th places (27·7 points whereas Opponent I can only discard two 5ths (20 points) and Opponent II a 6th and a 7th (24·7 points); however other competitors will also have a better chance of getting into the first three places.

The results of one race are often not available before the start of the next, and it is therefore essential to watch carefully to see where your opponents finish. Boardsailors have often directed their tactics against the wrong opponent because the results list was lacking. Mental arithmetic and a good memory are a great help, especially towards the end of a series when races are often run back to back, one immediately after the other.

Occasionally a boardsailor will give false information concerning his finishing place to avoid the attentions of a particular opponent, and if you feel this may be the case you can ask others who were nearby where he crossed the finishing line.

Up to now I have managed to avoid taking paper and pencil with me to the last race of a series, but if a good many competitors are all in the running this could well be the only way of deciding before the start which opponent you must keep astern regardless.

I may perhaps have made too much of the question of points, from the novice's point of view, but competitors sailing in the middle and back of the fleet are often keen to finish ahead of a particular opponent, and these comments about points situations are valid wherever the boards finish. Battling to defend 46th place can be just as tense as fighting to win a series outright.

	1st race		2nd race		3rd race		4th race		5th race		Total	Discard	Less discard
Your score	4th	8	3rd	5·7	1st	0	6th	11·7	10th	16	41·4	16	25·4
Opponent I	3rd	5·7	5th	10	4th	8	5th	10	1st	0	33·7	10	23·7
Opponent II	1st	0	4th	8	6th	11·7	2nd	3	7th	13	35·7	13	22·7

Formalities

A boardsailor intending to take part in a race or series must advise the organizers in writing before the closing date for entries. It is best to fill in an entry form, but the information can be provided without using a form, and the usual details required are name, address, nationality, club to which you belong, age, weight, type of sailboard and sail number.

Entry fees that have to be paid before the closing date should be sent with the entry form. Some race organizers set great store by this, and I have known even well-known boardsailors refused permission to compete in an important race because they had not paid up at the right time. I consider it fair to insist on the payment of the entry fee, or to make a supplementary charge for late payment. Racing is organized mainly by sailboard clubs whose arrangements and expenditure are based on the number of entries received; entrants may not turn up at the last moment because of bad weather or flat calm, but the organizers cannot be blamed for this and they should be spared from making a big loss.

In view of the continuous rise in the number of competitors, race organizers will doubtless soon limit the number of entries accepted for a race, depending on the venue and the wind conditions; the date the entry is received could be the deciding factor as to who will race, and obviously it would then be inadvisable to wait until shortly before the closing date before sending off the entry form and fee.

Preparations at the race venue

GETTING TO KNOW THE LOCALITY

When taking part in a weekend series, the competitors generally turn up a few hours before the first race, but it is better to arrive some days early when it comes to a longer and more important series, to have time to become acquainted with the area. Local conditions vary enormously from place to place; waves build up differently, winds shift unexpectedly and the tidal streams where the course is laid have to be considered. You must become familiar with the waters, and the local topography; you need to find conspicuous objects on shore that can be used as landmarks during the race. Note where changes in the colour of the water indicate differences in depth and try to study the local winds.

It is particularly important to arrive in good time when races are run in a different climate, because the body takes some time to acclimatize and adjust to the unaccustomed temperatures and the new environment. When racing in the tropics, a boardsailor from waters where there is little ultra-violet radiation should allow about a week to get used to the stronger sun; it takes at least that long before you can sail for longer periods without protection from the sun, the rays of which are reflected by the water, which virtually doubles their effect on the skin. Thin, light, plastic clothing provides the best protection against sunburn; oil only gets smeared on to the board and makes the surface slippery.

ACQUIRING INFORMATION

When racing in waters that are new to you, the first thing to find out is exactly where the course will be laid. A chart of the area to be used is helpful, and shows the shape of the coast, depths, shallows, currents or tidal streams nearby etc. Once you know where the course will be (or already is) laid you can start to build up a picture of how the wind is likely to vary in the sort of variation you can expect in the direction and strength of the wind.

FACTORS THAT AFFECT THE WIND

The wind is steadier when it blows over a smooth level surface, be it land or water, and the longer the distance it travels without interference the steadier it will be. This means that wind will be relatively steady when the area from which it comes is either a large expanse of water or flat land with no trees or buildings. On the other hand, if there are hills, woods or many buildings to windward the wind is likely to be gusty, and the effect of this will be seen by the varying colour of the water and the darker patches which sweep over it when the wind gusts.

THE PATTERN OF THE WIND

During the first sail in unfamiliar waters, the main object is to get some idea of the character of the wind. If you beat dead to windward and use conspicuous objects on shore as markers, you can discover how far the wind shifts by noting how much you have to alter course. This cannot be established with any great accuracy; it is more a question of forming a general picture which will help you later when deciding what tactics you should use.

Shifts in wind direction occur at certain intervals, determined by the object that causes the shift. The pattern of the shifts can be established gradually over a period, and as the board beats towards a blanketed area the shorter the interval between shifts becomes. The wind not only changes in direction but it varies in strength, and another point to establish is whether strong gusts always blow from the same direction, or whether they come from different points of the compass.

When weather conditions are reasonably stable, variations in wind direction and strength follow an almost rhythmic pattern, which is repeated more rapidly on the leg from the lee mark to the windward mark. If you can establish this pattern you will be able to make decisions as to when to tack or gybe with greater confidence.

You can make a quick sketch of local topographical features, such as a peninsula or hills which permanently divert the wind from its general direction. Wind always takes the path of least resistance; air rises ahead of an obstacle and returns more slowly to ground or sea level beyond it. The area that is affected to leeward of the obstacle extends up to six times the height that the wind rises vertically. Even a simple sketch shows how such variations will occur, but remember that this holds good only when the general wind direction is relatively steady.

How the wind is affected by obstacles on shore.

Gusts and eddies to leeward of a high coast.

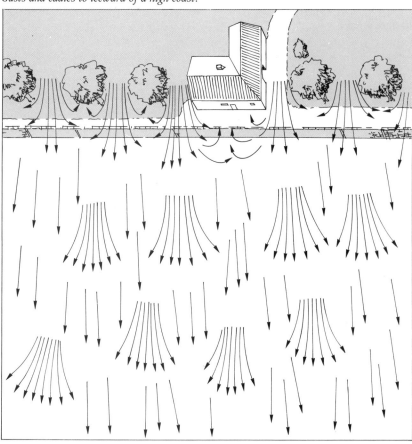

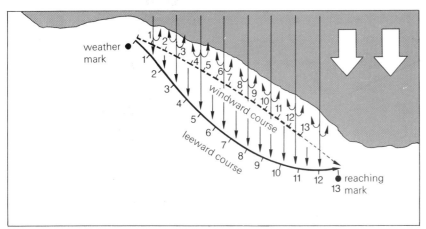

Above: Wind strength increases with distance from the windward coast.

Left: Deflected wind near the shore.

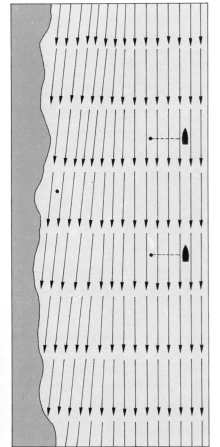

You may find that geographical features cause considerable and constant variations of wind strength on the course, and it is then often possible to make a detour on a particular leg to sail at a higher speed in undisturbed wind. For example, if the coast near the first reach is steep it could pay to sail a course to leeward of the direct line between the marks to benefit from the stronger wind further from the blanketed area.

Along the coast and on larger inland lakes, there are often areas where there is a noticeable and constant deflection of wind direction, even though the wind appears to be steady. These areas generally run parallel to the shore and extend 100–500 metres from it, even when the wind is blowing directly along the line of the coast. The wind is deflected a few degrees from its general direction to blow towards the shore, as in the figure left which shows this area by the shore and the marks of a triangular course.

THERMAL WINDS

Thermal winds frequently occur on lakes and along coasts with mountains nearby. For example on Lake Garda in northern Italy, which is the Mecca of alpine boardsailors, there is a near certainty of enjoying winds of over Force 4, provided that the weather is fine and stable. When the sun shines for a long period a thermal wind blows on hills and land near the water, because the air above them is warmed and rises, drawing cooler air in horizontally either from above the water where atmospheric pressure is higher owing to the lower temperature of the air over the water, or from shady north or east slopes. Thermal airflow is orbital, because when the air is cooled at a greater height it is then drawn horizontally to where it can sink again on account of the lower temperature.

A thermal wind pattern of sea and land breezes occurs daily along the coast, and is limited both in extent and duration. When the sun warms the land, the air above the land rises while the air over the cooler water sinks, and the circulation of the air results in a wind which blows from the sea towards the land during the day – the sea breeze. At night the opposite occurs when the land cools rapidly and the air above it sinks, whereas the water holds heat longer and the air above it rises. At night air flows from land to sea – the land breeze.

The angle at which the sun strikes the land greatly affects thermal winds, whether in mountainous regions or along the coast. As the angle becomes more acute when the sun is sinking, the land rapidly becomes less warm. This is why thermal winds on south coasts, and on the northern shores of lakes with a mountainous hinterland, are stronger and set in earlier.

The attraction of areas where thermal winds prevail is the certainty with which their strength and direction can be predicted, and the probability that they will exceed Force 2. The basic requirement for a good thermal wind is a fine, stable weather situation, with no strong high altitude winds. Information about what winds can be expected is best obtained from local sailors and boardsailors.

THE WEATHER SITUATION DURING THE RACE

If you are to have the right equipment with you when starting a race, you must have a rough idea what strength of wind to expect, and a weather forecast or map is a help. Provided that the course is not laid where thermal winds prevail due to nearby mountains, but in an area where the land is flat, you can assume that the strength and direction of the wind will be much as predicted in the weather forecast. Other important information can be obtained from a weather map or forecast as well:

- The position of high or low pressure areas, and the directions in which they are moving.
- The approach of warm or cold fronts, and their anticipated time of arrival in the area.
- Probable wind shifts resulting from the movements of a high or low.
- If thunderstorms are expected.

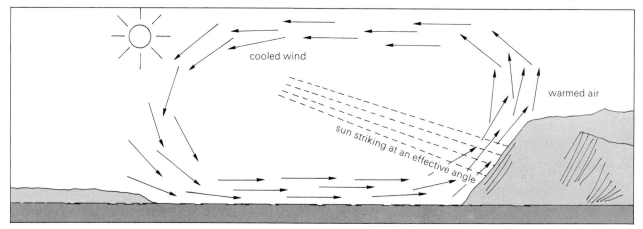

Thermal winds.
The principle of the sea breeze.

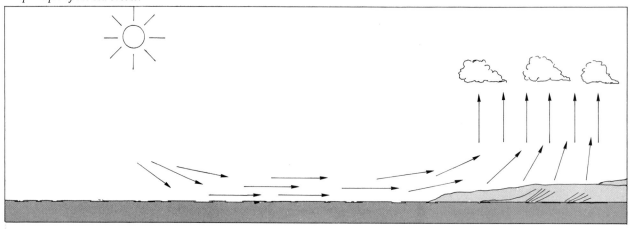

- How much cloud there is likely to be. Thermal winds may perhaps not set in because the sky will be overcast.

Although most sailboard races last no longer than an hour or two, and it is generally possible to return to the shore between races to change a sail or centreboard, it is important to form your own ideas as to how the weather will develop by watching the clouds. If the wind is relatively constant in direction and clouds are sweeping past, the wind will usually freshen soon after every large cloud passes, and then ease again as the cloud draws away. Right beneath the cloud the wind direction stays unaltered, but it is deflected outwards to either side. Thus, if the wind is basically from the west and a large cloud passes to the north of an area, the freshening wind will be from a more northerly direction but it will revert to westerly when it eases.

Clouds, towering higher, warn of a change in the wind.

How larger clouds deflect the wind.

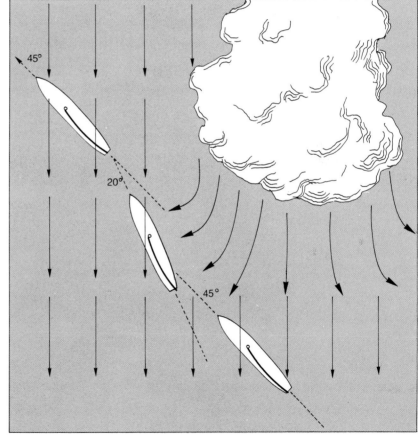

CURRENTS AND TIDAL STREAMS, AND THEIR EFFECT ON STRATEGY AND TACTICS

Another factor to take into account when considering racing strategy and tactics is the horizontal flow of water. In some areas this is slight and can be ignored when sailing purely for pleasure, but during a race good use must be made of any advantage it brings while adverse effects must be avoided or kept to the minimum.

There is no current on many inland waters, but occasionally there are localized eddies near the areas where water flows into or out of a lake. For example there can be a noticeable effect when a river flows into a lake near the weather mark.

In tidal waters the strength and direction of the ebb and flood stream vary hour by hour, and it is vital to obtain as much information as possible about them from publications and from local boardsailors. The times of high and low water are given in tide tables, often in the local newspaper, and sometimes in the sailing instructions as well. The boardsailor can establish from these times what the set rate of the tidal stream will be during the race in the area where the course is laid.

In many waters, the strength of the tidal stream increases with the depth of the water and if the chart shows considerable variations in depths where the race is to be sailed, the varying strength of the tidal streams must be taken into account. In order to make full tactical use of a tidal stream it helps to enter its direction and strength on a chart or a rough sketch of the course in much the same way as sketching in the winds that can be

expected. You can then decide broadly which course to sail, basing your strategy on the fact that it pays to stay in the area where the rate is least when sailing against a foul tidal stream, and to sail where the tidal stream is running most strongly when it is fair. You can see this in the figure on page 65. The moment to tack for the windward mark has to be delayed until the mark is aft of the line perpendicular to the board's centreline when the tidal stream is foul, as in the figure, and the

greater its rate the further you must sail beyond the mark before going about to fetch the mark. On the broad reaches the board should point some way to windward of the reaching and lee marks to allow for the set of the tidal stream. Were the tidal stream setting in the opposite direction, the boardsailor would tack for the weather mark before it was at right angles to the centreline, and on the broad reaches he would have to head to leeward of the reaching and lee marks to allow for set.

The rate at which a tidal stream sets increases with the depth of the water.

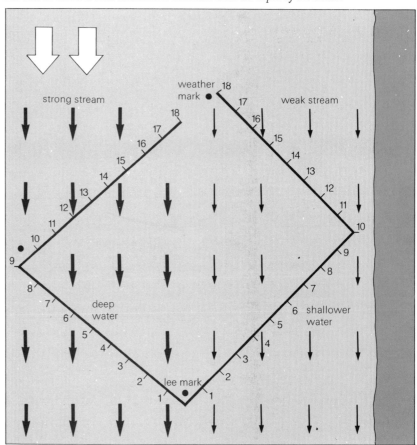

The direction in which a tidal stream is actually setting can be checked from the way an anchored object, such as a buoy or a ship, lies, as well as on beacons or posts which stand on the sea-bed.

SKIPPERS' MEETING

Every competitor is given a copy of the sailing instructions so that he has all the vital information that he requires to take part in the race. There is often a skippers' meeting as well, so that the race officers can explain any special points in the sailing instructions, and give details about the locality and the running of the race. The instructions should be studied thoroughly before the skippers' meeting so that any queries can be raised. Some of the important questions to which you must know the answers are:

- Will the starting signals be made at five minute intervals? Or will some other time interval be used?

- Will the various weight groups or classes start in succession, or will the whole fleet start together?
- How long is there between the finish of one race and the start of the next?
- When the fleet is divided into groups and there is a general recall, will that particular group be the next to start, or wait until after all the other groups have started?
- Where are the marks? How can they be identified?
- Is the starting line at the lee mark and the finishing line at the weather mark, or are they separate?
- What marks indicate the ends of the starting line?
- Is the Rounds the Ends Rule in force for the first start, or only after a general recall?
- If there is a general recall, how long will it be before the next signal is made?
- Are boards that are over the line at the start recalled individually, or will race officers simply fly flag X?
- Are wet suits and/or buoyancy aids compulsory?
- What are the race committee's views on pumping?
- What time does the first race start?
- Is there a limit before which the leader must have finished?
- What is the exact time shown by the clock which will be used to start the races?

The sailing instructions and the way the skippers' meeting is run enable you to judge how efficient and able the race officers are. Good, confident officers will start the races on time, even if only a handful of the entrants have reached the starting area, the starting line will be correctly laid, and the signals will be made punctually, strictly in accordance with the rules. No information

Avoid a contrary current or foul tidal stream; use a fair one that is setting you towards your objective.

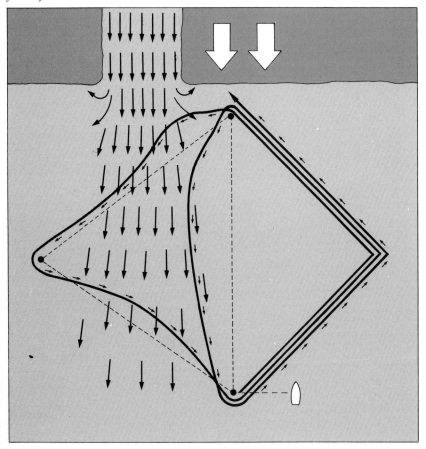

will be available from the committee vessel apart from what has already been given to all competitors because, officially, race officers are only permitted to reply to questions by means of flags to avoid giving any competitor an advantage. Efficient race officers will also abandon a race that has been started incorrectly, and will note down and recall or disqualify those boards that are on the wrong side of the line when the starting signal is made. Once the competitors discover that there will be a general recall if they fail to start correctly, they become more careful and there is then less likelihood of further general recalls.

Some of the signs of weak and indeterminate race officers are that the starting line is biased, signals are inaccurately timed and, instead of having the courage to protest against and disqualify competitors who break the rules, they shout such comments as 'Come on, get behind the starting line', or 'Stop pumping'. There may even be no general recall in spite of the fact that a mass of boards crossed the starting line too soon.

It is as well to form an opinion of the race officers' efficiency, because you will then know what you are likely to get away with. They may, for example, see two sailboards collide; if neither makes a protest the race officers have the right to disqualify both from the race. It is also important to know whether there is radio communication between the committee boat and the boat at the other end of the starting line; if there is not you may well be able to find a better starting position at the far end, hidden from view by other boards' sails. You cannot be identified by the race officers if you cannot see the bow of the committee boat.

CHOICE OF EQUIPMENT

After the skippers' meeting there is usually very little time to decide what equipment to use, and you should therefore make up your mind beforehand which sail and centreboard will be preferable. If you are unsure up to the last minute, be ready to rerig quickly. When the wind strength is very variable the ideal solution is to have a second complete rig assembled ready to use in strong winds.

When you decide what equipment to take, the vital factor is what the competitor whose points total is nearest to your own has chosen. When wind strength varies greatly, ranging from Force 4 to 7 and changing about every hour, it often pays to wait for the competitor that could still be beaten to rig his sail and to trust to luck by taking the alternative size. This is certainly the best answer when you have to finish a good few places ahead of him in the last race to make up the difference in points, but if both boards have much the same points total, the choice of sail size and mast stiffness should be governed only by the strength of the wind that is expected. On the other hand, if you are ahead on points and there is a real risk of being unable to control the larger sail, it is better to avoid ending up with a discard and to use the rig that is easier to handle.

Just before a race it is generally difficult to decide which sail to use, and I have often seen boards being rerigged three times when a strong gust could be seen whipping over the water, followed soon afterwards by a lull and then another gust. First and foremost such problems are easier to solve when you know from experience which centreboard and which rig can be used in a wind of a certain strength, and the more acutely you are aware of your limitations the easier the choice becomes. Your decision as to whether to use a harness or not also depends on up-to-date information on what strength of wind to expect.

CHECKLIST

Before setting out:
- Are the centreboard, skeg and the underside of the board really smooth?
- Does the standing surface provide a good foothold, or do you need to rewax it?
- Have you made figure of eight knots in the ends of the downhaul, kicking strap, outhaul and the line that holds the mast to the boom to prevent them from slipping right out of the cleats?
- Is the mast tip straight inside the mast sleeve?
- Is the uphaul attached to the mast foot?
- Have you rigged the safety line that connects the rig to the board?
- Are the harness lines made fast properly?
- Have you secured your watch strap so that it cannot open accidentally?

After setting out:
- Is the mast foot firmly in the step?
- Are the harness lines attached in the correct position so that the pressure is applied at the right point?
- Are the centreboard and skeg free of seaweed or long grasses?

PREPARATIONS ON THE WATER

Set out for the first race early enough to arrive at the lee mark about half an hour before the start. First check the positions of all the other marks and, if they are hard to find against the light or because of waves, look for some marker which will show the direction of the windward mark when you start off on the first beat. In particular, check whether there are similar buoys or floating objects nearby which could be mistaken for the weather mark during the hectic first beat. Many a victory has been won because the fleet followed a leading board to the wrong buoy, while one brave sailor who had been careful to check beforehand was first to round the correct mark.

This happened to me in the first race of the Windsurfer World Championship at Bendor in southern France. After the initial beat and the first broad reach I lay seventh, while the eventual champion, Matt Schweitzer, led the group of six, who were mainly Americans, about 30 metres ahead. About 50 metres from the shore there was a buoy which marked the limit of the area where motor boats were not allowed, and the lee mark was hidden from view by a spectator boat. I had identified it during the first broad reach and, when the leading group sailed about 25° too far to leeward towards the limit buoy, I luffed up sharply after gybing, on to the direct course to the spectator boat until the lee mark came into view beyond it after I had sailed about two-thirds of the leg. Many of the boards astern of me also followed the leading group and only realized their mistake very late. I therefore had a good lead when starting the second beat and was able to hold on to it until the finish.

Warming up before the start.

If you have enough time, it pays to beat from the lee mark to the weather mark to check whether the pattern of the gusts has changed, and, in particular, to note the wind conditions at the weather mark if it is close to land; you can also check whether your information about the tidal streams in the area is correct. During the run back to the start, offload your muscles and relax generally.

Sometimes the race officers cannot avoid laying the course in waters where there are obstacles, such as fishing nets or masses of seaweed, that are difficult to make out. Keep a sharp eye open for such pitfalls, and note their position so that you do not suddenly find you have to alter course to avoid them during the beat. Obstacles of this sort can be made use of when planning how to attack a board ahead of you; time your tacks so that your opponent will have to sail straight towards the obstacles if he is to stay ahead and keep you in his wind shadow, and you will then get clear when he is forced to alter course (see also section Attack on page 102).

4 The race itself

The start

Sailboards start a race 'flying' by crossing an invisible starting line with limit marks at either end, and sailing towards the first mark. The first leg of a triangular course is to windward and, ideally, the line should be laid exactly at right angles to the wind direction. The boards that start at the starboard end of the line then have an advantage in that they have a clear wind and are able to go about immediately on to port tack.

When the starboard end of the line lies a little further to leeward than the port end, this advantage of freedom to manoeuvre is virtually cancelled out by the fact that a slightly greater distance has to be sailed from that end, and any position on the line is then equally good. Should the wind veer before the starting signal is made, the starboard end will be further to windward and the preferable end of the starting line. A board starting there not only has freedom to tack but also starts further to windward. If the wind backs before the start, the port end of the starting line is better and the advantage, in terms of distance to windward, is shown in the figures on the right and opposite.

The aim is to be at the most advantageous position with a clear wind and

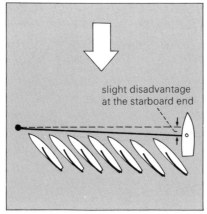

Above: An almost unbiased starting line.

In each case grey is in the best starting position.

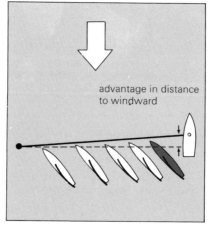

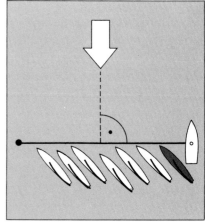

very close to, but not over, the line when or immediately after the starting signal is made, ready to cross the line at maximum speed to sail towards the windward mark.

Although there is a widespread misconception to the contrary, it does not matter which end of the starting line is nearer to the weather mark; the important point is which end is further to windward.

When the wind is fluky, its general direction in relation to the starting line has to be established so that you can find out which is the more favourable end, and this has then to be checked several times before the actual start. This is done by sailing to the middle of the line and bringing the board to a dead stop. When all way has been lost, hold the rig by the uphaul alone, with the mast as upright as possible over the centreline; the sail will then indicate the direction of the wind, and you can see whether one or other of the limit marks is further to windward. Repeat this procedure at both ends if the starting line is over 100 metres long. Hold the rig like this for at least 15 seconds and make sure that there are no obstructions to windward which would deflect the wind from its general direction, and that the board is making absolutely no way – any motion through the water would affect the direction of the wind acting on the rig.

Alternatively, when the wind is relatively steady and the starting line is over 100 metres long, the better end of

Checking whether the starting line is at right angles to the wind.

B starts at the end of the line that is nearer the mark, but A starts at the better end of the line because the port end is further to windward.

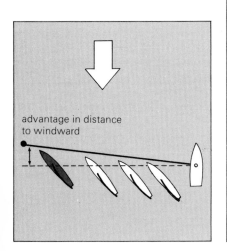

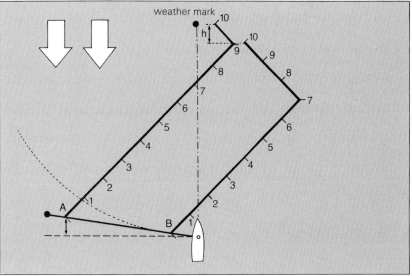

the line can be found with the help of another boardsailor. If the boards start from the limit marks at either end of the line, and sail close-hauled towards each other, it is easy to decide which end is more advantageous from their relative positions when they meet. I have always found someone willing to do this with me because we both benefit equally, but it is essential that both sailboards perform comparably when close-hauled.

Watch experienced racers when they are checking how the line has been laid. Often, once they have established which is the better end to start, they sail off to the other end to mislead their opponents, and they then stay there until there is only enough time left to sail to the place where they have decided to start. It is therefore not necessarily best for a newcomer to racing to follow at some expert's heels with a view to starting in the best place, albeit in the second row.

Many competitors do not take the trouble to determine the whereabouts of the most favourable position, and simply sail to the area where most of the other boards are congregating. This herding instinct often causes considerable congestion and, if you see this happening, it is particularly important to check whether the other end is perhaps more favourable after all so that you can start the first beat not only with freedom to manoeuvre but also with the advantage of being further to windward.

Once you have decided where to start, find out how much time it takes to reach that position, either by drifting down to it from windward or by sailing along the line on a beam reach. Try to keep clear of other boards as long as possible so that you do not

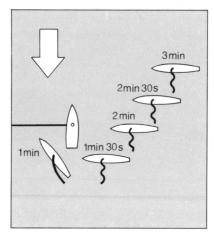 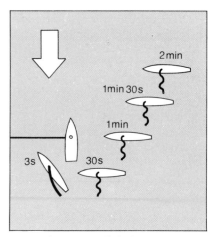

Timing the start in moderate to fresh winds.   *Timing the start in a light breeze.*

arrive in the thick of the crowd until the very last moment.

When the starting line is badly biased, bringing a marked advantage at one end, a great mass of boards will collect to windward of the extension of the starting line, and will drift down slowly to the limit mark. In light winds the speed of drift is generally overestimated and, when the starting signal is made, there will be many competitors still on the wrong side of the line who were not able to round the limit mark or the committee boat in time. I therefore recommend reaching the ideal position rather earlier when the wind is light, and to stay there by sailing stern first briefly. In medium and strong winds, competitors tend to underestimate the speed of drift and the mass of boards has often passed the limit mark before the starting signal, leaving a convenient gap into which you can slip at the optimum starting position. In moderate breeze and in strong winds especially, it is better to wait alone slightly to windward, or on the extension, of the starting line to see

how the crowd fares, and whether a small space appears for you close by the limit mark, just before the starting signal.

When the line is considerably biased, it can sometimes be better to start in a second row close by the limit mark where you can get a clear wind, than to be to leeward of the fleet right from the start, in the other boards' dirty wind.

Should you find yourself in the thick of the fleet, try to leave yourself a little space to leeward. You need to be able to swing the end of the boom around freely so that you can sail backwards and brake. The end of the boom could otherwise catch on a competitor's feet or on his mast foot, and if the wind is over Force 2 and your board has been making way slowly, the sail will be hardened and you will accelerate, quite unable to slow down or stop. The usual consequence is that you shove other competitors forward too, and so start a chain reaction which could quite possibly lead to a general recall.

The first important rule at the start therefore is: **Maintain freedom to manoeuvre.**

In strong winds especially, avoid coming into contact with other boards at the start because, if you fall or lose control of your rig, you will probably affect several neighbours to leeward.

When the port end of the line is the more favourable, the decision whether to risk a start on port tack depends on what the other boards are doing. When a great throng can be seen approaching on starboard tack soon after the preparatory signal, you can expect them to be at the limit mark when the starting signal is made, and a board on port tack will then have no opportunity to work clear of them. However, if there are only a few making for the line close-hauled on starboard, you can either pass astern of them at high speed, or go about on to starboard tack at the right moment to reach the limit mark first with right of way.

You may intend to start by sailing along the line and, if so, I recommend you to find a landmark on shore that it is in line with the starting line. You will be able to stay safely to leeward of the starting line if you keep this landmark to windward of the limit mark. You will be faced with many decisions to make, particularly when starting in this way: Can I overtake to windward of the board ahead or will I then risk touching the line and maybe infringing the Round the Ends Rule? The person who can sail most accurately along the line is absolutely certain to have a clear wind because nobody is able to get to windward of him to blanket him. Do not use your landmark initially, however, because it is a well-known fact that, when there is a large

During the last few seconds before the start the line seems very narrow.

fleet and a long starting line, the boards in the centre hang back. The distance between these boards and the line is usually between one and five board lengths, and you just make a mental note that this space exists so that, at the right moment, you can start to make way and cross the line with the starting signal. If the line has no bias you can gain a considerable advantage in this way, especially in strong winds and, if you leave yourself space to leeward, you will be able to bear away just before the signal and cross the line at maximum speed.

Anticipate that the wind may shift at the last minute and make all your planning worthless, and check whether the starters at the opposite end of the line have had to alter course suddenly; for example they may perhaps no longer be able to stay on starboard tack. On more than one occasion I have found that a wind shift of over 20° a few minutes before the start has turned a carefully thought out advantage into a considerable disadvantage. The first person to notice a shift, and to sail as far as possible towards what has become the better end of the line, will reap an advantage over those in the fleet that react sluggishly. A shift in wind direction can be observed sooner when it affects a boat that is some way to windward; you might see that a yacht sailing hard on the wind on starboard tack can point considerably higher, and you can reasonably expect the wind to veer and, consequently, the starboard end of the line may then suddenly become the more favourable. You need some sailing experience and the ability to interpret the signs if you are to be able to draw conclusions about the direction of the wind from the courses sailed

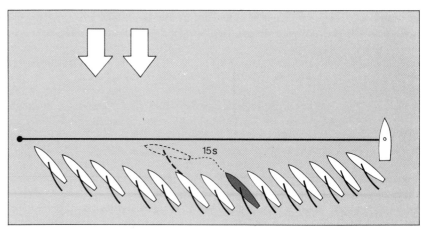

Starters hang back near the centre of a long line; during the last few seconds before the starting signal, sail clear of the line of boards and aim for the line itself.

Waiting for the starting signal.

by other craft, but this is nevertheless one of the few ways of spotting an approaching wind shift while it is still a good way off.

When drifting and waiting, watch out for sudden gusts which could accelerate your speed of drift and put out your timing. When the wind freshens, the crowd will suddenly be driven to leeward considerably faster, and you should try to stay clear as long as possible to give yourself a better chance of finding a gap between the limit mark and the other boards.

When the wind is very light, there is always the possibility that it may drop completely, and if there is any sign of this happening get to the position where you intend to start in plenty of time.

The second important rule at the start therefore is: **Watch out for and expect changes in the direction and strength of the wind.**

As you approach the line, check your landmark repeatedly to be sure that you are in the right area because sailboards sometimes form an imaginary starting line. It is easy to forget to check the position of the real line, and find yourself too far to leeward.

The race officers on the committee vessel may discover that the line has become biased owing to a wind shift, or that they have anchored out of line with the limit mark, and they then frequently try to reduce or eliminate the bias or correct the error by veering more anchor cable or shortening its scope. I have seen this done on a number of occasions, even after the preparatory signal has been made and, naturally, this ruins all plans as to where and how to start. Check from time to time that the starting line is still in line with your landmark, and keep an eye on the committee boat to see if someone is busy with the anchor cable.

The third important rule at the start is: **Avoid collisions!**

The last minutes call for increased concentration. Do not let yourself be diverted. There is no time for chat. Should you collide with a board, get clear quickly and do not get involved in an argument. If you think about other things, even briefly, you will find all of a sudden that there are only seconds to go before the start.

The boards in the centre are hanging back some distance from the line.

Signals

Flag and sound signals are made by the race officers on the committee boat to indicate the passage of time at the start of a race. Under the IYRU racing rules, if a race is not going to begin at the advertized time the international code answering pennant is broken out and a sound signal made, generally with a gun or foghorn, to indicate that the race is postponed and that the warning signal will be made one minute after the pennant is lowered. If the answering pennant is hoisted over one ball or shape, the first race has been postponed for 15 minutes, and the addition of a further ball or shape extends the postponement for a further 15 minutes.

The warning signal is often made by breaking out the class flag, but some other distinctive signal or flag may also be used, such as the flag which indicates to which side the marks are to be left. The class flag indicates which class or weight group will start first, a green flag sends the fleet off to sail clockwise round the course, leaving all marks to starboard, and a red flag indicates that all marks must be left to port; this is easy to remember because both the flag and port wine are red.

Normally the time interval between the warning signal and the preparatory signal is five minutes, and flag P, the Blue Peter, is broken out at the exact second, but sometimes the sailing instructions specify a three minute interval between signals. The racing rules and any special rules printed in the sailing instructions come into force when the preparatory signal is made. This is the very latest time at which to confirm that your watch coincides exactly with the time indicated by the race officers. Check the position of the second hand or the number of seconds shown on a digital watch so that you know the exact second to expect the starting signal.

Flag I is broken out one minute before the start if the Round the Ends Starting Rule comes into force, and means that any board on the course side of the starting line or its extension during the minute before the starting signal must return to the pre-start side of the line across one of its extensions before starting; in other words, he must return outside one or other of the limit marks and then start in the normal way.

If the Round the Ends Rule is not in force, a board is allowed to drift down to leeward during the last few seconds from a position just to windward of the line, and will be to leeward of the line only when the starting signal is made, Often, when a number of boards decide to start in this way, some do not drift to leeward of the line in time, and either they are recalled or there may have to be a general recall. After a general recall, the one minute Round the Ends Rule almost always comes into force, and may be altered by the race officers into three or five minute rule, provided this has been specified in the sailing instructions.

Flag P, flag I and the class flag are lowered and a sound signal is made to start the race. In the case of all signals made by the race officers, the visual signal takes precedence over the sound signal and, if you do not hear the gun

The last minute before the start of a tandem race.

Visual signals take precedence.

fire at the time that the start is due, check whether the flags have been lowered because that is the signal which indicates the correct time to start.

INDIVIDUAL RECALL

When one or more competitors have infringed the Round the Ends Rule or have started prematurely, the race officers break out flag X and make a long sound signal to inform them. The sail numbers of boards that have jumped the gun are rarely called out, and each boardsailor has to decide whether he has started correctly or not when he sees flag X. The flag is lowered when every board that was on the wrong side of the line has returned to the pre-start side of the line.

Boards returning to cross the line after a premature start do not have right of way and must therefore keep clear of those that have started correctly. When the Round the Ends Rule is in force, they rank as having started only after they have returned outside the limit buoys and then crossed the line correctly.

Instead of breaking out flag X, the class signal is sometimes left hoisted at the dip, halfway up the staff, but the meaning is unchanged. The responsibility for returning when recalled rests solely with the competitor concerned.

GENERAL RECALL

When the race officers are unable to identify the boards that start too soon, the first substitute, a blue and yellow triangular flag, is broken out, accompanied by two sound signals, to signal a general recall, but if you hear two guns, keep on sailing towards the weather mark until you can see clearly that the general recall flag is being flown from the committee vessel because I have known gunshots from a nearby wood mislead an entire class.

The race officers will also abandon the race if an error has been made in the timing of the start, and the entire fleet then have to return to start again.

After a general recall, check immediately whether you chose the right place to start before the other competitors start altering course to return to the line. If you sight at right angles to your centreline when close-hauled and the fleet is spread out all along the starting line, you can decide quickly whether it would have been those who started at the port end or those at the starboard end who would have been able to stay on course without having to give way when they met other boards. Amend your plans for the next start, but remember that the majority of competitors will also probably intend to start at the same place and anticipate that there will be even more crowding than before.

You will now discover whether you were listening properly at the skippers' meeting. How long will it be before the next start? Sometimes the sailing instructions specify only three minutes, but a new warning signal may well be made after a considerably longer interval. Watch to see whether the race committee alter the starting line with a view to avoiding another mass premature start and, if they do, check again to find which is now the better end.

As soon as you have clearly identified the general recall flag, return to the committee boat. When racing on Lake Forgges in 1979, 90% of the starters ignored the recall signal and beat on towards the windward mark. In the meanwhile, the few who returned to start correctly set off ten minutes ahead of those who had to run back and cross the line later.

The race officers were in the right; there is no rule to say that they must wait until all the boards have returned and are ready to start. Should race officers accept a start as valid because everybody has ignored their general recall signal, and there is then a protest against their action, the consequence will inevitably be the retrospective abandoning or cancellation of the race.

Right of way rules

Extracts quoted verbatim from the IYRU racing rules are printed in italics in this book, and the noun yacht is used because the rules, which are also used for sailboard racing, were drawn up long before the sport of boardsailing was invented. The right of way rules must be observed from the preparatory signal onwards. The following are the most important and are relevant at the start:

- Rule 36: *A port-tack yacht shall keep clear of a starboard-tack yacht.*

- Rule 37.1: *WHEN OVERLAPPED. A windward yacht shall keep clear of a leeward yacht.*

The overlapping windward boardsailor must keep clear by luffing up when, *sighting abeam from his normal station*, he is abaft the mast of the leeward board. Once the windward boardsailor is abreast of or forward of the leeward board's mast, the latter

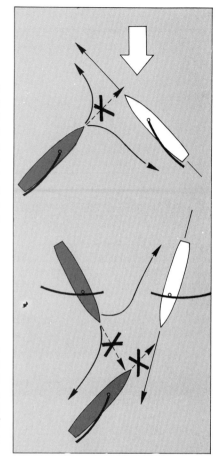

Rule 36: Port tack gives way to starboard tack.

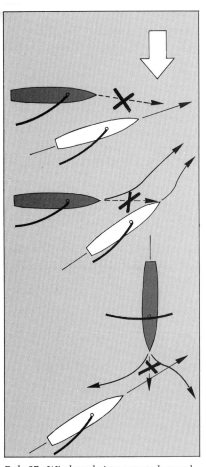

Rule 37: Windward gives way to leeward.

may not luff above a close-hauled course (before the start) or sail above his proper course (after the start), and the windward board may bear away again. Rule 37.1 is somewhat restricted by rule 40 in that, before a competitor has started, he may only luff slowly and in such a way as to give the windward competitor room and opportunity to keep clear and thus to avoid a collision.

● Rule 37.2: *WHEN NOT OVER-LAPPED. A yacht clear astern shall keep clear of a yacht clear ahead.*

A board may therefore not approach the fleet from astern and bump into competitors ahead, or perhaps push them over the line. Frequently a boardsailor approaches the better end of the starting line, and tries to force his way between the limit mark and boards waiting close by during the last

few seconds before the start. If a collision occurs, he will clearly have infringed the rule.

Nor may the limit marks be touched. The sailing instructions state whether the marks limiting the line will be two buoys or the committee boat and a buoy. The anchor cable and ground tackle, and anything attached only temporarily or accidentally to the mark, is not part of the mark as defined

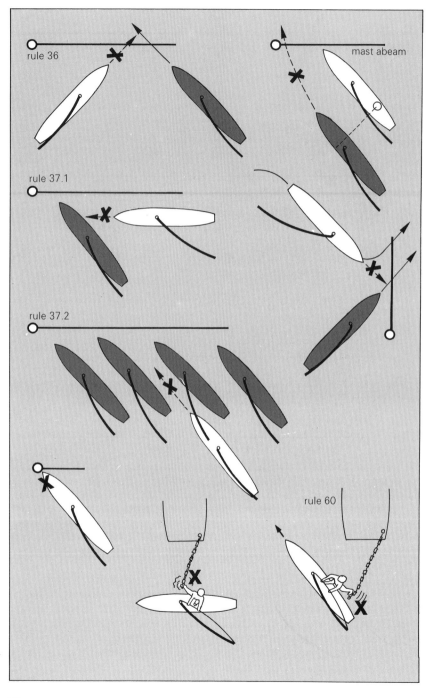

in the rules, and can therefore be touched, but the boardsailor may not shove himself off from it because this would break rule 60 (Means of propulsion). If a limit mark is touched, disqualification can be avoided by rerounding it after starting, but again the boardsailor must keep clear of all boards starting correctly, and may only return to reround it when he can do so without hitting or hindering any other board.

In spite of all the rules and the fact that rule breakers can be protested against and disqualified, there are times when insisting obstinately that you have right of way does not pay off as well as making a realistic appraisal of the situation; for example it pays to recognize the hopelessness of starting alone on starboard tack and taking on the rest of the fleet, all on port tack. I once had the audacity to try to insist on my right of way against some 40 competitors in an important Windsurfer race in Austria. The port end of the line was slightly preferable, and almost all of the boards had assembled there, having decided to start the first beat on port tack. In a wind of about Force 3, I approached slowly on starboard tack just before the start but when the crowd started to gather way my shout of 'Starboard' had no effect. I could not luff up to windward without crossing the line too soon, there was no space to leeward, and by the time that I had hauled my rig out of the water they were all about 50 metres ahead to windward. Oh yes, I was in the right, but that was no consolation because my protest involved only two competitors and had no effect on my finishing position.

Racing rules which apply before the start.

Some of the boards starting on port tack will have problems.

In accordance with Appendix 3, rule 1, a competitor that has broken one of the right of way rules can avoid disqualification by making a 720° turn; he must make the two 360° turns at the first reasonable opportunity, but if a rule is infringed before the start the turns are made after the starting signal and before starting. Just as when returning to cross the line after being recalled, or when rerounding after touching a mark, the boardsailor has to keep clear of all other competitors.

If another board has broken a rule, the right of way boardsailor can ask him to make a 720° turn, and the need to make a protest is avoided if the board acknowledges the infringement by performing this alternative penalty. A boardsailor may still lodge a protest, even after the other board has made a 720° turn, if he feels that he has been seriously and deliberately hindered by the infringement. Another reason for protesting to the race committee would be that a collision resulted in damage sufficiently serious for the right of way competitor to have been at a disadvantage when continuing the race, or to have been forced to retire.

The 720° turn alternative penalty has been very widely adopted. On a short course the distance lost while making the two turns is so great that the right of way competitor who has been hindered can almost always finish the race ahead of the rule breaker.

Anybody may have to make a 720° turn, however carefully he tries to comply with the rules, and it is therefore only sensible to practise performing this alterative penalty. In a light breeze, the time taken can be cut to a minimum if you turn the board round beneath you with your feet while swinging the rig through 360° the opposite way. The end of the boom should be close above the surface, but it can be dipped into the water from time to time to increase the turning effect. In moderate or stronger winds, the sailboard will swing round quicker if weight is shifted to the edge that is on the outside when making the turn.

Gate start

An alternative method of starting competitors off on the first beat is with a gate start. Some sailing boat classes have found that this is the only way to prevent an endless succession of general recalls, and this method of starting may well soon be adopted by sailboard race organizers too, because the continuous growth in the number of competitors greatly increases the probability of mass premature starts.

The principle is that one competitor, selected before the race, sails close-hauled on port tack; the direction of his course forms the starting line, and the speed at which he sails determines the rate at which the gate opens. The pathfinder selected is often the person who was the last of the first fifth of the finishers in the previous race.

The signal which indicates that there is to be a gate start is often flag G, which is flown on the anchored committee vessel. Signals are made as for a normal start, except that there is no Round the Ends signal one minute before the starting signal. The pathfinder waits near the committee vessel, together with the gate boat which has race officers on board.

The time that the pathfinder sets off depends on the strength of the wind, but will be during the last minute before the starting signal is made. The gate boat motors about three lengths dead astern of him, and a second motor boat may accompany them, staying ahead and slightly to leeward of the pathfinder where race officers on board can observe the competitors and keep them clear of him. Three seconds or so before the starting signal the gate boat drops a dan buoy with a white

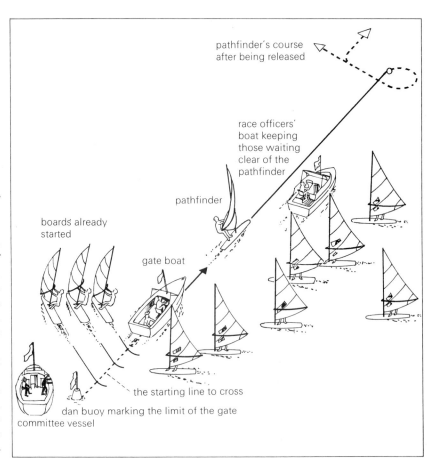

Gate start.

flag, usually marked G, and the line between this buoy and the centre of the gate boat's stern forms the starting line, which all competitors have to cross on starboard tack. The gate opens progressively as the boat motors in the wake of the pathfinder, who is released after some minutes. He starts the race after gybing on to starboard tack round the stern of the gate boat, which continues at the same speed and on the same course until the gate is wide enough, and then drops a second dan

buoy with a white flag to indicate the starboard limit of the starting line. Stragglers can start belatedly anywhere along the line, and may do so until flag G is lowered, accompanied by a sound signal, to close the starting line.

A competitor is disqualified if he touches the gate boat or the pathfinder after the preparatory signal, or stays on the port side of the gate boat and interferes with the starting process. No alternative penalty is permitted, a board cannot be recalled, and rule 13.3 may be amended by the sailing instructions so that qualified competitors are also excluded from a race that has to be re-started.

- Rule 13.3: *Rule infringements in the original race shall be disregarded for the purpose of starting in the race to be re-sailed.*

If a gate start is to work really well, the wind direction must be relatively steady because only then will conditions for the first competitors to start be the same as those for boards starting later and further to windward. Nevertheless, there are still advantages to be gained when this method of starting is adopted, and how to benefit depends on the conditions that prevail. You must always cross the line immediately astern of the gate boat at high speed, but whether it is better to start as soon as the gate is opened or to wait further to windward depends firstly on how the wind shifts and then on the pathfinder's close-hauled speed:

- If the wind keeps veering, and shifts to starboard, wait further away from the committee vessel and to windward, ready to be one of the last to start.
- If the wind keeps backing, and shifting to port, cross the line as soon as the gate has been opened, and go about as soon as possible to make use of the wind shift.
- If the pathfinder sails slower than you do when close-hauled, an early start gives you an advantage over

those who start later because you will already have made up ground on the pathfinder.

- If the pathfinder sails faster than you when close-hauled, wait to windward and start last, immediately astern of the gate boat, because you will then have less distance to sail on the first beat.
- When the wind is not steady and the speed of the pathfinder differs from yours, his speed is more important and should decide when you will start.

Experienced racers are not keen on gate starts because they enable almost all the competitors to start a race in an equally good position, and there is therefore little opportunity to benefit from making the right decision on where to start, as when a normal line is used. Furthermore, unlike a normal start, there is little prospect of the start failing and, consequently, much of the excitement and tension inherent in the start of a race is lost; to my mind this considerably reduces the fun of racing.

The first beat

After the rough and tumble of the start, it is important to make an appraisal of the situation which faces you. In the first few seconds after starting, you must be absolutely clear what alternatives are open to you. Do not let yourself get into an argument about some confusing occurrence at the start. There is only one thing that matters now: to get to the weather mark as quickly as possible.

Immediately after the start the situation is generally that a great many boards are on starboard tack, all trying to work a little further to windward by pointing better than the rest to get a clear wind. Because everyone is doing the same, the mass of boards makes slow progress. The first essential after the start is: **Get your wind clear.** Try to bear away into a gap to leeward to increase your speed and get a clear wind; then concentrate on sailing close-hauled at a good speed. Some-

Just after the start, many boards tend to sail too close to the wind.

times the fleet sails a very long first tack on starboard towards the left side of the course, simply because none of the boards to windward wish to go about and those ahead and slightly to leeward cannot do so without infringing the rules. As soon as one board tacks others follow suit, and the fleet gradually spreads out all over the course.

Do not clear your wind by tacking blindly to extricate yourself from a blanketed position. You must first check how you will be placed after going about. The second important rule after the start is: **Think ahead.** If you intend to tack from starboard on to port, make sure that you will not be forced to give way immediately to another board with right of way. Instead of tacking again it often pays to pass astern of several boards that are on starboard tack if your intention is to get a clear and stronger wind, or to take advantage of a wind shift. When you wish to cross between two starboard tack boards, the second of which is dead astern of the first, you can only do so if they are more than one board length apart.

The figure (right) shows a typical situation after the start. How can the various boards get a clear wind quickly? A is blanketed by B and C and, to get a clear wind, should tack as soon as D's wake has been crossed. B already has a clear wind, but can be luffed by C and must either try to work rather further windward by pointing higher or go about as soon as C starts luffing. E, in D's wind shadow, is in a relatively hopeless position and the only hope is to bear away to try to sail clear of D by increasing speed. However, as starboard tack board with right of way, E must not alter course to

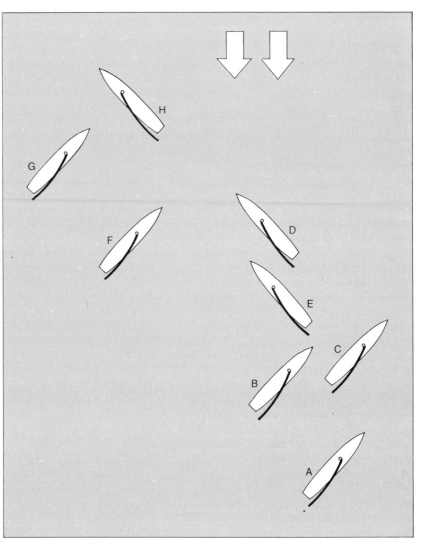

Possible situation after the start.

prevent F from keeping clear. F has to keep clear of both D and E, and should go about quickly to avoid being caught in their dirty wind. To pass astern of both would mean bearing away excessively, and this would be advisable only if it were absolutely essential to

make for the right hand side of the course. H is safely in the leading position, enjoying a clear wind. G should give away a metre or two, by bearing away with the sail slightly eased, to pass close under H's stern and obtain freedom to manoeuvre.

It is very rarely that the wind blows absolutely steadily from one direction, and the great secret of beating is to make use of wind shifts. Your trial beat before the start should have given you some idea of the way it is tending to back or veer.

When the average direction of the wind coincides with the direct line between the lee and weather marks, the rule is: **Sail on the tack which is at a more acute angle to that line.** Neither tack will be better if the wind is absolutely steady and blowing along the direct line; in theory, just two long tacks will take you to the windward mark. However, such a constant wind is the exception, and even the slightest of shifts will mean that one tack is at a more acute angle than the other. During the beat, should you find that you are going to have to bear away because the wind has headed you (blowing from a direction nearer the bow), and you go about instead, the angle through which you tack will be less than 90° as a result of the wind shift, and you will find that you are sailing at a better angle on the new tack, on a course that takes you nearer the weather mark. When you make use of every wind shift in this way, you will zig-zag your way toward the mark, with each tack at a relatively acute angle to the direct line between the marks.

It is often difficult to decide whether the wind really has headed, or whether it will shift back to its former direction almost immediately, but you learn from experience that you should not react at once to a change in wind direction that is accompanied by an increase in wind speed. Sometimes turbulence deceives you into thinking that the direction is changing, and it is therefore better to stay on your original tack for a few board lengths when the wind freshens so that you are sure that the wind really has shifted. If you are over-anxious to make use of every slight change of wind direction, you may find that the wind shifts back again almost immediately and, having gone about, you will then be caught head to wind.

The diagram below shows how much distance can be gained by making use of wind shifts; one of the

The lead gained by A as a result of choosing the correct tack each time the wind shifts. b has always chosen the wrong tack.

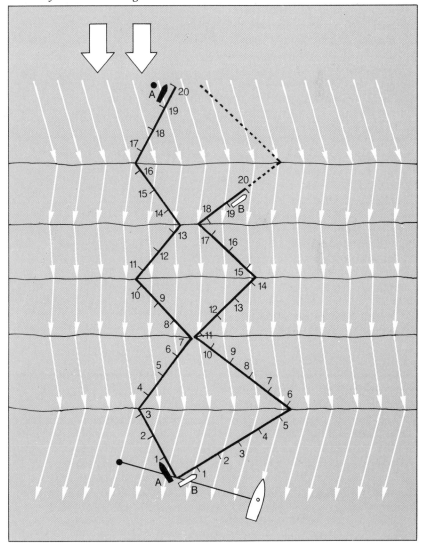

competitors has made good use of every alteration in the direction of the wind whereas the other has gone about each time at just the wrong moment. It is very noticeable that, when novices are beating, they often just seem to sail back and forth without actually making much progress towards the weather mark.

Frequently, it is far from easy to decide which is the better tack just after the start. Keep an eye open for gusts, and sail towards them because not only will you sail faster in the stronger wind but you almost always find that the wind will shift in a gust, and you can then use the shift to good advantage, as already described.

Changes in wind strength and direction can be spotted soonest by observing the effect of the wind on sailing boats, flags and smoke to windward. When you see that there will be a change the rule is: **Sail towards the direction from which you expect the new wind to blow.**

It then pays to abandon the tack that takes you towards the mark, and to sail to meet the fresher wind, especially when the breeze is light and you can see a thundery squall approaching from a different direction. The distance you lose initially by sailing a course that takes you further from the mark will be more than regained later because you will be sailing faster and at a better angle.

When one side of the course is close to the shore, you can rely on the fact that the wind there will blow from a rather different direction. If the line of the shore is parallel to the wind direction, the rough uneven surface on the land brakes the wind slightly, deflecting its general direction a few degrees towards the land. Again the

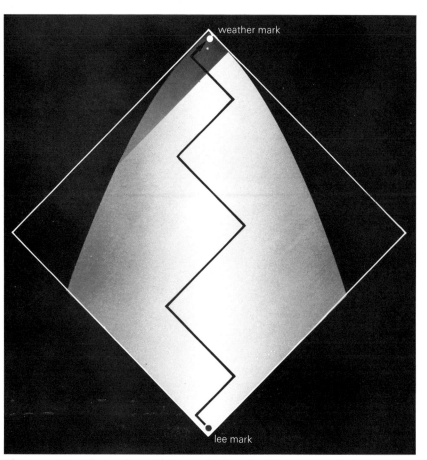

The surest way to the weather mark is near the direct line between the lee and weather marks.

wind will rarely be steady and will shift slightly to either side of the direction to which it has been deflected. Continue to sail on the tack that takes you towards the weather mark, and only leave this area nearer the shore when you can fetch the mark. However, when using the wind in this way it is advisable not to stray too far from the direct course, that is the straight line between the lee and weather marks. The figure above shows the area within which it is

usually best to stay during the beat; it can be seen that as the boardsailor approaches the weather mark he should stay closer to the direct line, and make rather shorter tacks to avoid having to sail further unnecessarily if the wind shifts again at the last moment. When beating in a wind that is shifting to a rhythmic pattern the rule, therefore, is:

Always stay on the tack that takes you towards the weather mark at an angle that is more acute than 45°.

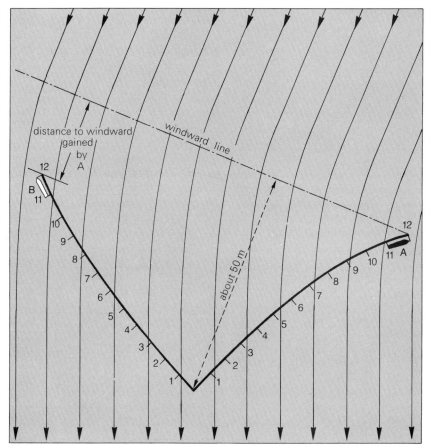

If the wind shifts gradually and steadily, sail towards the direction from which it will blow. If necessary tack to achieve this. The black board has gained over the white one in this way.

When the direct course between lee and weather marks does not coincide with the wind direction, the geometry changes somewhat. Establish before the start which tack will take you nearer to the weather mark and, once you have got a clear wind, stay on this tack until the wind heads you, at which point go about. Stay on this tack either until the wind shifts back again, when you should go about on to your original tack, or until you are able to fetch the mark.

If the wind starts to head you during the beat, and you are sure that it will head more and then blow from its new direction for a considerable time, you should bear away when it first starts to head and wait until it has steadied before going about; you will have gained a few metres to windward by comparison with those boards that tacked as soon as the wind started to shift. On the other hand, if the wind frees slightly and you expect it to free further before its direction steadies,

you should go about immediately, sail towards the shift, and stay on that tack until the wind has settled in its new direction in order to gain distance to windward over those boards that simply luff up.

It is not easy to decide whether a wind shift will last for a longer or shorter period and, when in doubt, it is advisable to follow the suggestions made for short-term shifts.

When you meet other sailboards

When you have to keep clear of two boards sailing on starboard tack, consider whether it would be better to pass astern of them both. If you go about in their wind shadow, you will lose speed and will only be able to tack back on to port after they have passed. If you are ahead of them, on the other hand, you can tack into the safe leeward position, just to leeward of at least one of them, and keep your wind clear. This is advisable only if you can sail at least as fast as they do when close-hauled. Do not go about too close to leeward of an opponent with a view to catching him in your dirty wind, because you run the risk of breaking rule 41.

- Rule 41: *A yacht which is either tacking or gybing shall keep clear of a yacht on a tack.*

Should you be on a starboard tack and wish to discourage an opponent on port tack from going about just to leeward of you, bear away in really good time and hail to inform him that he may pass ahead of you. He may then let slip this opportunity to go about into the safe leeward position, and to join you on your better tack.

If you are on port tack and suddenly hear a shout of 'Starboard' close by, you must act immediately to avoid a collision, either by luffing up and going about, or by bearing away to pass under the other board's stern. It is absolutely essential to keep a really good look-out to leeward; no rule requires a person to shout 'Starboard' – you, on port tack, are responsible for not colliding with or hindering any other competitor with right of way. The only way to avoid finding yourself blanketed by another board as a consequence of having had to tack hastily to avoid a collision is to keep an eye open all round, and to anticipate every possible situation that could arise.

The wind may be such that you want to make a long port tack and, if so, you should bear away when starboard-tack boards approach with right of way to pass astern of them; you can then luff up at greater speed to your proper close-hauled course.

Should you have established before the race that the tidal stream is foul on the windward leg, try to minimize its effect by beating to windward in shallower water, which is generally found near the land; on the other hand, when the tidal stream is setting to windward, benefit whenever possible from the stronger stream by staying where the water is deeper. Always remember to allow for the tidal stream, especially when approaching the weather mark. When it is fair you can tack for the mark earlier than at slack water, but if it is setting you to leeward, sail some way beyond the mark before going about; the stronger the tidal stream the further you should sail beyond the mark before you tack for it.

Approaching the weather mark

Provided it is possible in the waters where the course is laid, a race is generally sailed anticlockwise round a triangular course, leaving marks to port (red flag). The reason is that competitors that have tacked for the weather mark approach it on starboard tack with right of way, and it has been found from experience that the racing rules are broken much less frequently than when racing clockwise round the course. When all the marks must be left to port, check in good time, say when you have covered about half the first beat, whether there are likely to be many sailboards massed ahead of you at the weather mark. If this is the case, plan your beat with a view to approaching the mark on a rather longer starboard tack, assuming the wind direction allows you to do so. It is virtually certain that a long line of sailboards will be approaching the weather mark on starboard, and any boardsailor arriving on port tack would have to wait to find a gap through which to sail before he could tack for the mark. Normally you will have no chance of fetching the mark if you tack to leeward of them; you will not be able to point high because of their dirty wind and, being so near the mark, all the boards will be sailing really close to the wind.

Watch the other boards carefully so that you can decide when the right moment has come to go about for the last time on to the tack which will take you to the mark. Boards often overstand the mark by sailing too far before going about, and you will realize that they have done so if you see them sailing towards the mark at a rather higher speed with sails slightly eased. Provided you have a clear wind, do not sail beyond the wake of a sailboard that will clearly be able to fetch the mark but, if you are caught in another board's wind shadow, sail a few metres further to be absolutely sure that you will pass to windward of the mark. A great deal of time is wasted if you have

to wait close by the buoy for the fleet to pass, and for a gap in which to tack because you were unable to fetch the mark.

When a boardsailor is in close pursuit, and is checking to see whether you, having gone about, can lay the mark so that he can tack for it himself at exactly the right moment, you can mislead him by bearing away slightly just when he crosses your wake. You will give him the impression that you cannot quite fetch the mark, and he

will then stay on the other tack a few moments longer thinking that you will have to go about again twice, but you just luff up again and round the mark without putting in the extra tacks.

If no board is following you closely, play safe by overstanding slightly to ensure that you will round it, even if the wind shifts a little or if you make more leeway than you expect.

Should you decide that you will not be able to fetch the mark after all, and there are many other boards close by,

18525 must go about immediately.

put in a short tack as soon as you can to avoid losing time while the long procession makes its way to the mark. However, if you have plenty of room, wait until the last moment before tacking because there is a chance that the wind may free and allow you to luff up and make the mark after all; if it stays steady, tack when you are really close to the mark because you can then see exactly how long your extra tack must be.

When the race officers fly the green flag and all marks have to be left to starboard, you will decide at some point that the time has come to go about because you will be able to lay the weather mark on port tack. Check first how many starboard-tack boards you are likely to meet and, if you are going to have to give way to a fair number, stay on starboard tack until you are beyond the point where the mark is at right angles to your centre-line – you will then be able to round it without having to put in an extra tack after passing astern of the right of way boards.

Rules that apply when rounding the weather mark

Rule 36 (Port tack keeps clear of starboard tack) applies in the vicinity of the mark at the end of the beat, as does rule 41 (When tacking or gybing keep clear of a board that is on a tack). Beginners are particularly likely to infringe rule 41 when near the weather mark. A board must not go about just to be able to call water immediately afterwards either:

- Rule 41.2: *A yacht shall neither tack nor gybe into a position which will give her right of way unless she does so far enough from a yacht which is on a tack [whether port or starboard] to enable this yacht to keep clear without having to begin to alter course until after the tack or gybe has been completed.*

The tack is completed when the board has borne away, when beating to windward, to a close-hauled course; if not beating, to the course on which her sail is filled. A gybe is completed when, with the wind aft, the sail, having crossed the centreline, has filled on the other tack. Until that happens a competitor without right of way must keep clear.

Should the mark be touched, disqualification can be avoided by re-rounding it and, while exonerating himself in this way, the boardsailor must keep clear of those boards that are about to round, or have already rounded, the mark correctly.

Anyone touching the mark must reround it.

Rule 41.2: Gybing and tacking.

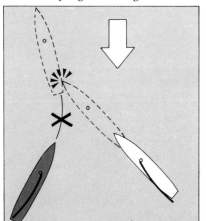

After the weather mark

The reaching leg

Once the first beat is behind you, half of the opportunities that are open to you during the race have gone. The tension over wind shifts and right of way rules eases slightly, and I always feel somewhat relieved when I have finally rounded the weather mark safely.

You can make a quick review of the race so far. Did you make serious errors which you could avoid on the next beat? Have you established a characteristic pattern of wind shifts which could help you to anticipate them next time? How fast did your opponents sail close-hauled? Would it be better to point rather less high on the next beat, and so increase board speed?

As soon as you have a quiet moment after rounding the weather mark, trim your sail to the new course, whether it is a beam reach, a broad reach or a run, by adjusting the outhaul and kicking strap. Ease the foot until a vertical crease appears close by the mast, and then harden the kicking strap until the crease disappears again. The further off the wind that you will be when sailing to the next mark, the fuller your sail should be. It is best not to adjust the trim of the sail if your course will be closer to the wind than a beam reach, and there is a possibility that you may be involved in a luffing match.

You may find yourself in one of a number of situations after you have rounded the weather mark:

1. With no competitors several board lengths ahead or astern of you.
2. With a crowd of boards close ahead of you.
3. With a crowd of boards close astern of you.
4. Hemmed in by a number of boards.

In situation 1 you are free to concentrate fully on board speed and wind shifts. Given a constant wind of Force 3 or less, bear away immediately on to the direct course for the reaching mark but, if the wind is stronger, sail a few metres on a beam reach before bearing away on the first large wave, removing the daggerboard or raising the centreboard if necessary. If there is a temporary lull in the wind, stay longer on a beam reach so that you can sail towards a fresher gust. Initially you will make less ground to leeward, but this will be more than made good when you bear away to sail faster in the gust, and you will also benefit from reaching the stronger wind sooner and accelerating earlier. Make longer use of the fresher wind by bearing away beyond the direct course between the weather and reaching marks until the gust eases; although you will sail a greater distance your speed will be higher, and

you will make more ground to leeward. Luff up again as soon as the wind eases so that you sail towards the next gust.

Your tactics in situation 2 depend on the actions of the boards ahead. If they start to luff up sharply, regardless of the fact that they are sailing towards a lull, bear away and try to get far enough to leeward of them to break through their wind shadow with the help of the fresher gust. You will not succeed in breaking through unless the distance you are to leeward of them is about equal to the distance over which the bunch of boards is spread. Should the wind then ease slightly, you must luff up to sail towards the gust so that you meet it at the same time as the rest of the boards. Once the first half of the

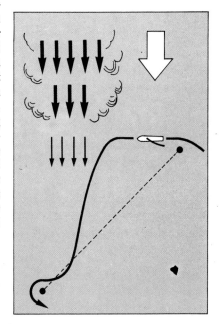

Sail towards the gusts, and bear away to stay in them.

The only way to overtake a group of boards like this is to sail round them.

Rule 39: The leading board may not bear away below her proper course when the overtaking board is within three of its overall lengths.

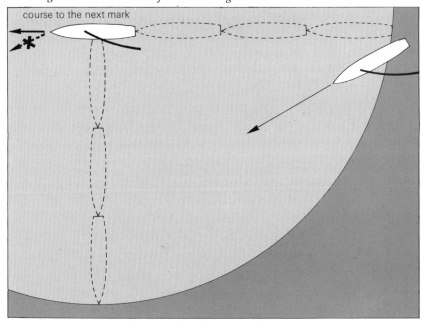

reaching leg has been sailed, boards are less likely to try to prevent an opponent from overtaking by luffing violently, but you can still benefit from sailing towards a gust, and the advantage gained may enable you to catch up or overtake the boards ahead.

On the other hand, the boards ahead of you may bear away immediately on to the correct course, and when the wind is constant or increasing you should stay longer on a beam reach to get far enough to weather of them for there to be no danger of your being luffed. You have a better chance of reducing their lead and catching them up when you have a clear and fresher wind.

Situation 3 is the most critical. Boards will try to overtake you both to windard and to leeward, but you

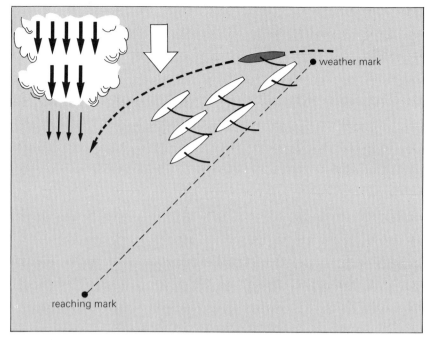

should concentrate on preventing any board from sailing to windward of your wake, even if this causes you to luff above the direct course to the reaching mark. After you have rounded the windward mark luff up rather more to discourage the boards astern from attempting to overtake you to windward. As soon as you find that nobody is trying to overtake to windward, you can settle down and concentrate solely on board speed. If you stay to one side of, but as close to, the other boards as possible, they will not be able to break through your wind shadow. You must however comply with rule 39.

- Rule 39: *A yacht which is on a free leg of the course shall not sail below her proper course when she is clearly within three of her overall lengths of either a leeward yacht or a yacht clear astern which is steering a course to pass to leeward.*

A proper course is defined as *any course which a yacht might sail . . . in the absence of the other yachts affected, to finish as quickly as possible . . .* The proper course is frequently the direct course to the next mark, unless there is some intervening obstruction, or a strong tidal stream to allow for.

Should an opponent nevertheless succeed in crossing your wake and attempt to overtake to windward, you can defend yourself by luffing.

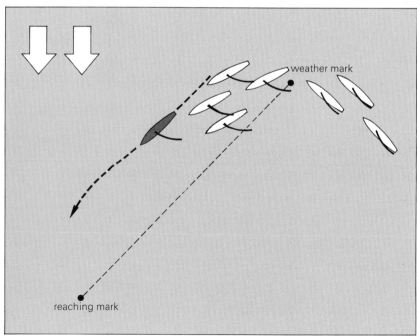

Left, above: The broad reaching leg when there is a bunch of boards ahead.

Left: How to sail the broad reach when there are several boards astern.

- Rule 38.1: *LUFFING RIGHTS After she has started and cleared the starting line, a yacht clear ahead or a leeward yacht may luff as she pleases subject to the proper course limitations of this rule.*

- Rule 38.2: *PROPER COURSE LIMITATIONS A leeward yacht shall not sail above her proper course while an overlap exists if, when the overlap began, or at any time during its existence, the helmsman of the windward yacht (when sighting abeam from his normal station and sailing no higher than the leeward yacht) has been abreast of or forward of the mainmast of the leeward yacht.*

A board with luffing rights may luff sharply until head to wind, and the boardsailor is not obliged to warn the opponent of his intention to luff but, to be fair, I feel it is best to warn the other board by calling 'Luffing' or 'Water' to catch his attention. The helmsman of the windward board must hail 'Mast abeam' or words to that effect when he reaches that position, to stop the leeward board luffing, and they then bear away on to the proper course.

Situation 4 is more difficult to resolve successfully because you have to consider the actions of the boards ahead and of those astern. Get to windward of the group and stay there unless you have a good chance of succeeding in breaking through to leeward, but remember that, if you do bear away, you will immediately find yourself in the wind shadow of the boards astern and, initially, will not have the best of wind conditions. If you decide to luff up, keep far enough

Rule 38.1: Luffing.

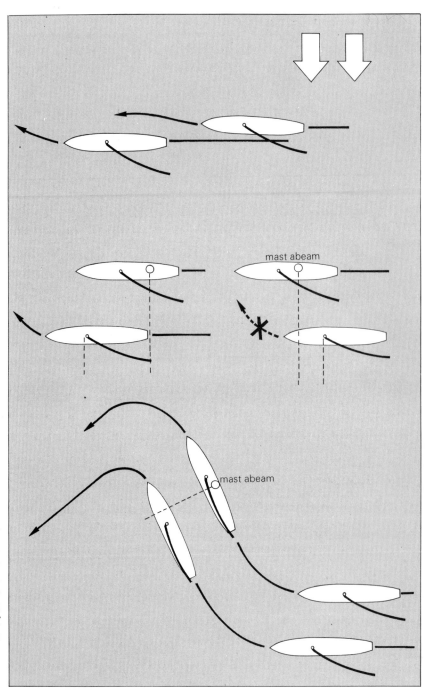

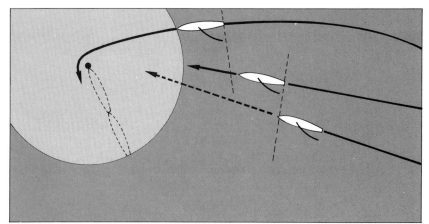

Rule 42: Overlap at the mark.

F85 must keep clear of 111 as the latter rounds the mark (Rule 42.1).

away from a board to leeward to avoid becoming involved in a luffing match. Defend yourself against overtaking boards as described above (situation 3) but do not get carried away and sail such a detour that you lose all contact with the boards ahead of you.

The rules relating to boards overlapping at marks are very important at the reaching and lee marks:

- Rule 42.1(a): *An outside yacht shall give each yacht overlapping her on the inside room to round the mark . . .*

- Rule 42.3(a): *A yacht clear astern may establish an inside overlap and be entitled to room . . . only when the yacht clear ahead is able to give the required room and is outside two of her overall lengths of the mark . . .*

A board is clear astern when abaft of a line at right angles to the other board's stern or equipment in normal position. The other board is clear ahead. They overlap when neither is clear astern; or if, although one is clear astern, an intervening board overlaps both of them.

When you are on this first broad reach, and marks are to be left to port, try to establish an overlap in good time by getting to leeward of opponents ahead of you. The course shown in the figure on page 94 is ideal and you will start the second broad reach in a good position, to windward of your opponent.

Should you fail to obtain the inside position, give your opponent the very minimum of room so that the mark is very close to leeward of him when he has to gype. It may even pay to ease out your sail after gybing round the mark on to the new course, so that you can luff up immediately astern of him.

Although you will lose a little ground, you will start the next broad reach better placed to catch your opponent more quickly in your wind shadow and blanket him.

When the two reaching legs are at the same angle to the wind, you can use the same strategy and tactics on both, but one leg may be at a considerably more obtuse angle, and will then be nearer a run than a broad reach. Do not allow yourself to be tempted into a luffing match which would take you far to windward of the direct course, because you would then have to bear away and run down to the mark, and your speed would obviously decrease. Just as on the running leg, the important point is to make ground to leeward. If boards try to overtake you, bear away to leeward where their wind shadows will be smaller, and wait until later before luffing up to increase your lead over following boards by sailing faster.

When you have a quiet moment and expect life to become too hectic to do so later, trim the rig ready for the next beat. This must be done before round-ing the lee mark. Never sail the last few metres with a really full sail; it is far more important that, when you luff up after rounding the mark, your sail is trimmed ready for the beat. Anticipate bunching at the lee mark and, at the same time as you retrim the sail, replace a daggerboard that has been pulled right out and push it halfway down, or lower a centreboard that has been fully raised at least halfway; shifting the centre of lateral resistance further forward will make it easier to luff up. Better still is to set the centreboard ready for the next beat while you are approaching the lee mark, provided the wind is not too strong to allow you to do this.

In a really strong wind, when it is impossible to approach the mark on a broad reach with the centreboard right down because the board would luff up unintentionally, place the daggerboard in the slot or lower the centreboard when you are a few metres from the mark, hold the rig by the uphaul alone, and let your board drift past. It is always preferable to round safely but slowly than to have the board luff up uncontrollably to windward of the mark at the last moment, and possibly hit it.

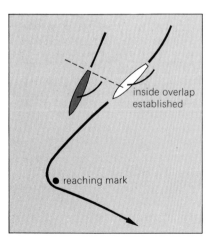

Rounding the reaching mark.

inside overlap established

reaching mark

Rounding the lee mark

The heading for this section could equally well be 'starting the next beat'; it is this that determines your tactics and strategy. The essential is to avoid sagging to leeward, because any ground that is lost means that there is a longer distance to cover close-hauled. On the first tack after rounding the mark, you should be to windward of the wake of opponents ahead of you, and it is therefore even more important to fight for the inside position at the lee mark than at the reaching mark. The boardsailor who rounds in the inside position will be best placed at the start of the beat that follows, and the ideal course to sail round the lee mark is shown in the figure on page 95.

You may approach the mark close astern of a bunch of boards, unable to establish an overlap, and it then often pays to ease out the sail momentarily so that you can luff up astern of the other sailboards and start the beat really close to the mark on the optimum close-hauled course.

You will benefit greatly when op-ponents close by hinder each other, but you must be sure to keep your own wind clear of any disturbance, and avoid getting too close to boards to leeward because, otherwise, you will sail a much larger circle and be unable to follow the ideal course when round-ing. It is far better to start the beat in a good position with a clear wind, free to go about at any moment, than to gybe quickly as you round in the outside position, because it is then virtually inevitable that you will be in the wind shadow of other sailboards when you start your first tack. The distance you gain with your slick gybe will have been more than lost a few board lengths later.

There may be a danger that boards ahead will collide at the lee mark, or that a rig dropped in the water will block your perfect course round the mark. In such cases, reduce your speed for a while because, when the wind is

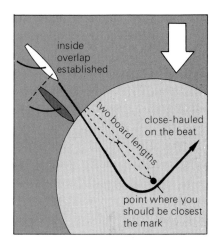

Right: Rounding the lee mark.

Below: Approaching the lee mark.

moderate or strong, the obstruction will drift to leeward very quickly, and it is more than probable that you will be able to squeeze through the gap left close by the mark. You should only risk sailing round the obstruction if you are really close to the buoy, and while doing so you must comply with the racing rules by keeping clear of a competitor who has lost control of his sailboard and is unable to get out of the way.

In your very first race you will discover, at the reaching and lee marks, whether you have practised rounding marks properly, and whether you can judge the turning circle of your board so exactly that you sail the perfect course round the buoy. If you find yourself dissatisfied, take an early opportunity to brush up your technique with more practise. You will soon prove to yourself that you can make up a lot of lost ground in a very short time when you round the lee mark perfectly.

The second beat

Your strategy on the second beat will largely be based on what you learnt and how your fared on the first beat, but the wind may well have changed completely in the meantime, and the opposite side of the course may have become preferable. Sometimes it is just bad luck that leads you to choose the wrong side of the course, but it helps to keep a close eye on those competitors that have already rounded the lee mark while you are still on the second broad reach. Can they point closer to the weather mark on one tack than on the other? Have they gained or lost ground as a result of a wind shift?

Plan your strategy for the second beat before you reach the lee mark, and concentrate on having a clear wind after you have rounded it. Your main aim again is to make the best use of wind shifts and gusts, except when there is a competitor with a points total so close to yours that you simply must keep him astern of you, or when somebody is trying to hold you in his wind shadow. The fleet will now be much more widely scattered, and it is not so vital to approach the weather mark on starboard tack in a situation where all marks have to be left to port.

F 102 should immediately sail to one side, clear of G 3131's wind shadow.

The run

When rounding the weather mark and bearing away from a beat to a run, sail as tight a circle round the mark as possible. If there are boards close astern you are then able to alter course immediately, away from the direction in which you expect them to sail. Should the run have become a broad reach owing to a considerable shift in wind direction, and you consequently have to make an alteration of course of over 135°, a stop gybe is best for the reasons just stated, but be sure that you are far enough away from the mark for the boom not to touch it as it swings round.

You can raise the centreboard or daggerboard partly or entirely when the sea is calm, the wind is light and no competitors are nearby. You will sail faster, without fear of a capsize fall, if you raise the centreboard fully, but you must then keep absolutely still because even the slightest movement of the board will nullify the advantage gained by reducing wetted area to decrease resistance. Trim the sail to increase camber; it should be even fuller than for a very broad reach.

While sailing the last few metres of the beat in a very fluky wind, try to decide on which side of the running leg you can expect stronger gusts to occur and, immediately after rounding, sail to that side of the direct line between the weather and lee marks, right ahead of the freshening wind. The more irregular and the more marked the changes in the wind the further can you risk deviating from the direct course.

When the wind is steady, and there are some sailboards no more than about ten board lengths ahead, you can concentrate all your attention on one of them, and blanket him carefully – by sailing dead to windward of him – to slow him down and gradually gain on him. As you get closer to him the distance between you will decrease more quickly because the effect of your blanketing increases progressively. If he tries to escape from your wind shadow, follow him unless you yourself are in danger of being blanketed by a board astern. He will try to get clear of your wind shadow by making violent alterations of course,

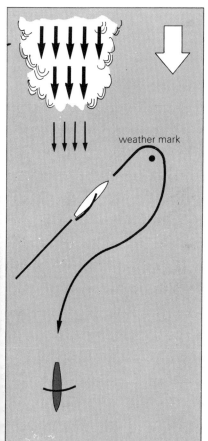

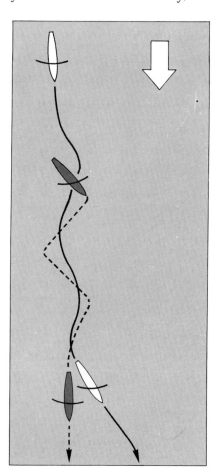

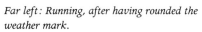

Far left: Running, after having rounded the weather mark.

Left: Blanketing when following a board on the run.

97

but you can turn more gently while keeping him blanketed, and these less abrupt alterations of course will also help to reduce the distance between you.

If you do succeed in catching up with him, alter course when you are no more than a metre astern of him, and sail at least three board lengths to one side, on the side that will give you inside position at the mark.

Should a following board try to blanket you systematically like this, sail a considerable way towards the direction from which you expect a fresher wind to blow. When running, it is vital to keep a good look out astern, firstly to keep an eye on and escape from sailboards that are in pursuit, and second to look for any alterations in wind strength so that you can make the best use of them.

You may have noticed during the beat that there is a constant alteration in wind direction on the second half of the run where it has been deflected by geographical features nearby. You should then sail the first half of the leg on a broad reach, roughly parallel to the direction that the wind will blow later, and this enables you to broad reach again on the opposite tack on the second half of the leg. In this way you will cover a slightly longer distance but will have the wind over one or other quarter for the whole of the running leg, and you will sail faster than those boards that start on a slow dead run with a very broad reach to follow, as well as those that start by broad reaching on the wrong tack and then have a dead run down to the lee mark.

Should a really strong gust strike when you are running, bend your arms a little, move your weight further aft and bend your knees. This is the best way to counter the increased pressure on the sail.

As you approach the lee mark, try to anticipate what will happen.

Try to establish an overlap by blanketing.

Rounding the lee mark after the run

The final beat

After the last mark has been rounded, you are unlikely to be able to improve your place when your opponents are skilled tacticians. If one opponent is determined to keep ahead of you personally, and knows all the tricks, it is very difficult to break through his defence on the beat. Your best chance of overtaking him is to blanket him on the run.

Should there be boardsailors just ahead of you at the end of the run, be sure to establish an overlap so that you can round the lee mark in the favourable inside position. You must start to alter course, which may involve turning more than 135° on occasions, at exactly the right moment to be placed just to leeward of the mark when you have close-hauled after rounding, without having given away even one centimetre to leeward. To achieve this your course will initially be quite some way from the mark, the distance between you and the buoy being determined by your board's turning circle. If you are not bothered by other boardsailors nearby, sail a wide curve so that you luff up from a fast reach.

When other competitors are closing on you, and are trying to establish an overlap just before you reach the mark, defend your position by luffing up and bearing away at the appropriate time. Luff up to close the gap to leeward of the mark so that a boardsailor who has not established an overlap and has slowed his board is unable to find room to work his way between you and the mark.

If you are approaching the mark without having obtained the inside position, you can ease your sail out briefly to slow down, so that you can try to slip in between the mark and the sterns of the other boards ahead, and will then be able to start the final beat without having lost ground.

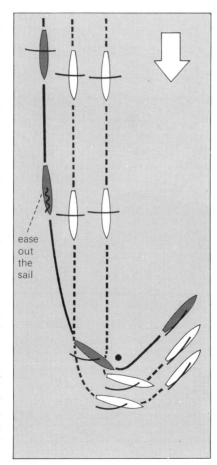

ease out the sail

DEFENCE

At the very latest you should have decided by the time you round the lee mark after the run on your strategy and tactics for the last beat. You may decide that you intend to maintain your present place, and that there is little prospect of improving it by passing boards ahead and, if so, your defence should be based on the principle: stay between the boards following you and the next mark which, in this case, is the finishing line.

When there is only one opponent that you need to cover, and he is less than five board lengths behind you, round the mark and do not tack until he too has rounded and gone about.

Left: Rounding the lee mark when astern of several boards.

Below: Rounding the lee mark at the end of the run.

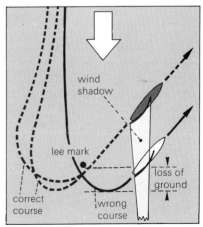

wind shadow

lee mark

loss of ground

correct course

wrong course

Point up really high after rounding the mark so that you catch him in your wind shadow. When he goes about, you should follow suit so that he stays in your wind shadow.

Should boards be further astern, go about when you have covered half the distance of your lead over them so that,

Right: 83371 is covering 82716.

Below, right: Defence during the beat.

Below: Go about when you have covered half the distance of your lead from the lee mark.

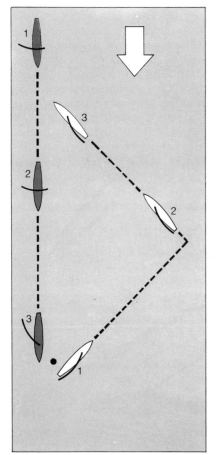

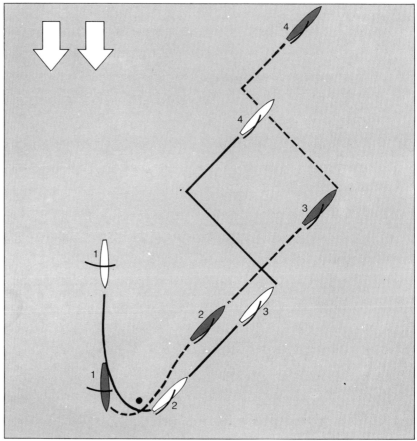

when they round the lee mark, you will be dead to windward of them, right on the direct line to the weather mark and ideally placed to cover them. If you follow the principle given above, every wind shift will reach you before your opponents; when the wind frees you can luff up sooner than they can, and when it heads, although you will of course have to bear away first, you know that they too will have to alter course almost immediately before tacking.

It is easier to defend your place against following boards when they are bunched together, because they then affect each other's wind and will consequently be sailing slightly more slowly, but they will spread out over the course soon after rounding the lee mark, and you must have already decided on which board to concentrate your attention. You will cover the one that affects your present points position, so check first which of your opponents is closest to your points total.

Towards the end of a series, there are always several defence/attack duels in progress concurrently. You may be covering one board but, indirectly, it is the board that is attacking him that will determine when you tack, because the board you are covering will himself have to tack to cover his attacker. Sometimes you can see a procession of boards all on one tack; when the board furthest to leeward goes about, there is a chain reaction and they all tack in turn to cover each other. It is relatively easy for you to defend your place against such a group because the boards stay bunched together but, if the group breaks up into individuals sailing widely differing courses, time your tacks to coincide with those of the board astern that lies just ahead of you on points.

It may be that the boardsailors astern sail considerably faster than you when close-hauled, perhaps because they weigh less or have better equipment, and it is then better not to cover closely but to try to hold on to your lead by making the very best use of wind shifts. Should they nevertheless succeed in catching up or overtaking you on the final beat, there are still several possible ways by which you can reach the finishing line first.

15 goes about immediately to get clear . . .   *. . . of E 22 by sailing to the other side of the course.*

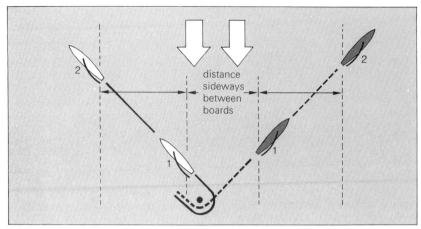

To have any chance of attacking successfully, there should be a considerable distance sideways between the attacking board and the defending board.

One board can defend his lead easily when the others are bunched like this.

ATTACK

When your opponent is using the defence tactics described above against you, first get your board to sail at least as fast as his so that you can break clear of his wind shadow. While he is sailing slightly to windward and ahead of you, he has to look back at you frequently to check whether you are still in his wind shadow, but you can see him constantly and will find that he usually checks at fairly regular intervals. Should you be within five board lengths of him, bear away immediately after he has looked back at you, accelerating to break through his wind shadow. You will of course lose ground to windward in consequence, but you cannot attack unless you have a clear wind.

If your board does not perform well enough when close-hauled for you to have a chance of winning such a duel purely by sailing faster and the points situation is such that you expect a certain opponent to cover you closely on the final beat, you should try to sail to an area where wind conditions are rather different by choosing the opposite tack to his as soon as you have rounded the lee mark. The further the distance sideways between you, that is the distance at right angles to the general wind direction, the greater your chance of finding somewhat different conditions. You have nothing to lose and can therefore risk dropping back further if the wind shifts to your disadvantage. It is better to stay on that tack until you find, when sighting at right angles to your centre-line, that you can cross ahead of your opponent. Provided that this is the only competitor who concerns you, it may even be best to stay on that tack and not go about until you are so far to one side of the course that you can lay the finishing line. Should you find that you cannot cross ahead of your opponent after all, or if the wind shifts back again before you have crossed him, go about again immediately when you are at an angle of 45° or more to the general wind direction.

Your opponent's actions will also affect your decision whether to tack or not. If you have had difficulty in getting clear, and anticipate that he will cover you closely as soon as you approach, stay well to one side of the direct line between him and the finish. You may want to get to the other side of the course where you expect conditions to be advantageous, and the only time you can dare to cross his wake is when he is being diverted by other sailboards, or is trying to hold on to his lead by sailing particularly carefully.

Should he succeed in covering you closely, there are other ways of getting clear. A wind shift always reaches an opponent ahead slightly earlier than it does you, but he has to wait for you before he tacks on the shift, otherwise you would get clear by not tacking; therefore, when the wind heads he has to bear away slightly whereas you stay pointing high until the moment the shift reaches you. Should you find that he goes about automatically at the same moment as you do, you can try to lead him into a position where he has to give way, preferably to several boards such as a bunch that are still on the run. Either he will have to stay on his original tack, leaving you clear of his wind shadow on the other tack or, after going about, he will have to bear away and lose some ground to windward to keep clear of the other boards.

False tacking: Close-hauled.

Luff up obviously.

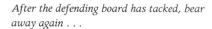

After the defending board has tacked, bear away again . . .

. . . on to a close-hauled course.

Another way of getting clear of his wind shadow is to make a false tack. Luff up until your opponent notices you doing so, and harden the sail vigorously and audibly; he will look round at you once and immediately start to go about himself. While he completes his tack you should bear away again to continue sailing on the old tack. This trick is usually only successful once because in future your opponent will wait until your bow has swung right round on to the new tack before he goes about. It is worth while practising false tacking, even though the opportunities to use it are rare.

You may find that your opponent goes about rather more slowly than you do, either because his board does not turn quickly or because he is less sure than you are and, if so, you can make a great many short tacks, gaining a little each time you go about and gradually closing on him. He may lose heart and allow you to sail away on the opposite tack to an area where the wind conditions are different.

Generally, however, you will be concerned with more than one opponent during a long final beat. It is relatively easy to keep control when you are in the lead, but if one board-sailor attacks boldly, and you have to take the risk that the wind will shift unfavourably while you are defending your lead you may find that other boards following at a greater distance astern may suddenly come very close.

Your tactics will depend on whether you can allow other opponents to overtake because their doing so would not affect your points placing. On several occasions I have found that a bunch of boards astern chose to sail what appeared to be a virtually hopeless long tack to one side of the course, and then finished up ahead of me while I was busy trying to stay ahead of one particular sailboard on the other side of the course.

Think ahead during the final beat, and do not forget to check on the boards astern. When you are short-tacking, especially, be careful that slowing down the tempo does not make all your hard work worthless when boards that have taken two long tacks suddenly appear ahead of the pair of you engaged in your private duel.

Close finish.

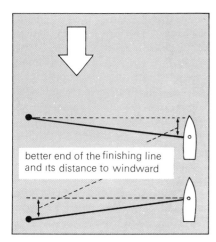

The finishing line.

better end of the finishing line and its distance to windward

Approaching a biased finishing line.

APPROACHING THE FINISHING LINE

When you are rounding the weather mark at the end of the second beat, whenever possible check carefully how the finishing line is laid. You will know whether there is a separate finishing line, or whether the windward mark forms one end of the line. What needs to be checked is which end of the line lies further to leeward.

As with the starting line, the finishing line is rarely laid exactly at right angles to the wind direction, but this time the better end is the one that is further to leeward because the distance to be covered to it on the beat is shorter than that to the other end (see figure left). Note which end is better, and time your last tack to fetch the finish at the point furthest to leeward. If you overstand, other boards can tack to leeward of you and will cross the line ahead of you as in the figure below. When you anticipate that a number of boards will reach the finishing line together, try to cross on starboard tack if possible, so that opponents on port will have to go about at the last moment, leaving you to cross the line ahead of them.

A board is deemed to be racing until the finishing line and marks are cleared, and a boardsailor on port tack must therefore keep clear of competitors with right of way until he is no longer racing. Should there be a collision, he can avoid being disqualified by making a 720° turn on the last leg of the course before crossing the line to finish and, to ensure that you are listed as finishing in the correct position, it is as well to point out to the race officers on the finishing boat that this has been done.

When there is a very close finish, your final chance of crossing first is by luffing up sharply about two metres before you reach the line so that the bow will touch it sooner; as defined in the rules, *a yacht finishes when any part of her hull or of her crew or equipment in normal position crosses the finishing line* . . . It is better to carry on close-hauled some way beyond the finishing line to be absolutely sure that you have crossed it and finished, as well as to avoid any possibility of drifting back on to a finishing mark after going about which can lead to disqualification.

When other competitors approach the line after you have finished, and their finishing places affect your final points placing, you can try to catch them in your wind shadow from a position beyond the finishing line, and

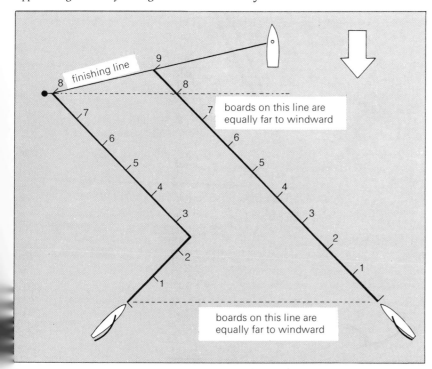

finishing line

boards on this line are equally far to windward

boards on this line are equally far to windward

this may allow other boards to finish ahead of them and so improve your points position. I succeeded in doing this at the Baltic Championships in 1977. In the last race I finished in second place and the boardsailor following me had to finish third if he was to win the championships. I was able to hold him in my wind shadow until he had crossed the line, while another board slipped past to finish third. This gave me just enough points to win the championship and was fair, but the situation was extremely tense to the final second.

Even if you have a really good knowledge of tactics and considerable experience, you find again and again that a great many of the sailboards that are ahead of you at the lee mark before the final beat are boards which you almost always manage to beat. In such a situation you have nothing to lose, and only desperation tactics can work miracles. By that I mean that you need to sail the last leg using quite different tactics from those that normally pay on a beat. You can take a flyer, that is to sail, preferably alone, right over to one side of the course, hoping that there will be a helpful wind shift which will enable you to fetch the finish on one tack after going about. You are most likely to benefit from taking a flyer when the wind shifts occur at such long intervals that you do not expect one until you have covered about half of the windward leg. When the wind is gusty and wind shifts occur much more frequently, staying on one tack like this would mean that you would sail considerably further than the sailboards that had used the wind shifts and made shorter tacks, and you would be unlikely to make up this distance after going about.

When you round the lee mark in the first third of the fleet, the rest of the boards will be running down towards you in the opposite direction. Avoid sailing into a mass of sailboards, because your wind would be disturbed. It does not matter if you meet a solitary board because the wind shadow only affects you for a very short time, and there is therefore no point in going about simply to avoid getting to leeward of a board that is on the run.

Shortening course

Flag S, displayed at the starting line, means that the shortened course prescribed in the sailing instructions will be sailed. An Olympic course is often shortened by omitting the run and the last beat, leaving only the first beat, two broad reaches and the final beat to be sailed. Other courses may be shortened in various ways.

It is even more vital to have a good start when the course is shortened because, with only two-thirds of the course left to sail, there are fewer opportunities to make up ground lost at the start.

The course is usually shortened because the wind is very light, and may well drop entirely during the race, but another reason could be that a violent thunderstorm appears probable, and the race officers are unwilling to risk the chance of competitors being struck by lightning.

Should the wind drop or a thunderstorm occur unexpectedly, the race officers can shorten the course after the race has been started by flying flag S at or near the finishing line, when the boards generally finish at the end of the round still to be completed by the leader, or at a rounding mark when it usually indicates that the sailboard will finish between that mark and the committee boat. The way in which courses are shortened varies, and the sailing instructions should be checked carefully.

When the shortening course signal is made at any time after the warning signal, flag S is displayed and two guns are fired or two sound signals are made to draw the attention of competitors to the fact that the course has been shortened. Sound signals cannot always be heard if the wind is freshening or the fleet is very widely spread, so watch out for the flag if the weather is such that you suspect the course may be shortened. When a final beat to the finish is all that remains of the race, base your tactics on the recommendations given in the sections on attack and defence (see pages 99–104).

Between races

After you have finished a race, watch the boards that follow you and ask yourself whether those that finish immediately behind you will affect your points placing, and whether some other boardsailor has suddenly improved his placing so much that his points total is now close to your own. Hammer the points totals of your nearest rivals into your head so that you know which boards to concentrate your tactics on when sailing the final beat of the next race. Should you find that there is only one boardsailor who is a threat, you can cover him systematically from the start onwards, as described in the section on the final beat (see page 99).

It is worth taking risks if the successful outcome of a series of races depends on finishing the last race really well placed. Depending on the circumstances you could try a port tack start, taking an extremely long tack on the beat, or sailing a course that is well to windward or to leeward of the others on the broad reaches. If you do succeed in sailing yourself into a satisfactory position, you should then change your tactics and concentrate on defence.

Watch, too, to see whether some of the competitors that are still beating to the finish have found a beneficial wind shift as a result of taking a long tack to one side of the fleet, and so gained a number of places. Although it is not always possible or advisable to use the same tactic in the next race, it always helps to know how your strategy might be improved.

Now is your opportunity to return to shore to make repairs or replace gear if your sailboard or equipment has been damaged in any way, but confirm first with the race officers that you have time to sail to the shore and back before the next start.

MUSCLE RECOVERY

Muscles become taut and your biceps and forearms get cramp when the wind strength is such that it is impossible to stretch your arms fully on the beat. When the wind is strong, symptoms of fatigue also occur and cause the forearm muscles to swell and become hard, particularly if the sleeves of your wet suit jacket fit too tightly. Back and calf muscles also suffer from cramp and

fatigue, your back muscles in particular in winds of over Force 5, but your calf muscles rather earlier in light to moderate winds owing to overloading the toes. If you have cramp, first remove tight clothing but do not expose cramped muscles to the cold.

If there is too little time to go ashore before the start of the next race, sit on your board and massage your forearms vigorously. Stand up from time to time, and swing your arms round alternately and quickly in vertical circles until your fingers prickle. Centrifugal force accelerates blood circulation, and the cramp will ease more quickly.

If you can sail to the bank, you may be able to take a shower. Hot water helps muscles release tension particularly quickly, and you should keep them moving afterwards. There are several pharmaceutical products, such as muscle and massage oils, which relieve cramp and have a loosening effect. The skin becomes really hot when they are rubbed in, and the muscles then relax more quickly. These oils also have a very good preventative effect and, if you rub them into the muscles that are worst affected before starting the race, the time at which your strength starts to diminish can be postponed slightly. Be especially careful to clean all the oil off your hands afterwards otherwise your hands will slip on the boom sheathing.

WARMTH

If the race was exciting, it is all too easy to underestimate how cold you will become after you have crossed the finishing line and need to rest. Once you start to get really cold it is much more difficult to warm yourself up again on the water. Cold wind on wet

skin lowers body temperature extremely quickly, and more body heat is lost when the water evaporates. The first essential, therefore, is to dry thoroughly all the bare parts of your body because they will become cold quickest. You can warm cold hands under your armpits, which are protected from the wind, or in the sleeves of your windproof jacket.

When the temperature is so low that you know you must expect to get really cold hands, you can extend the length of the period before they become painful by sailing about for some 20 minutes before the next start, until you feel the first signs of cold in your fingertips. Then warm them up, whether on the water or on shore, until it is time to get ready for the start. This will increase their blood supply and they will stay warm longer, especially if you can also keep them dry.

The moment that you feel the first signs of their getting really cold again during the race, take action immediately so that the pain which follows will not affect your concentration and mobility. When close-hauled, you can hang the elbow of your after arm over the boom to offload your hand, which you can then warm slightly by moving it about and clenching and unclenching your fist. Although this is certainly not the most efficient way of supporting the rig, there are races which are won by the person who concentrates on outlasting the rest of the fleet in spite of icy cold, rather than on obtaining maximum driving force from the rig. If the wind is light to moderate, you can hang both arms over the boom and rub your hands together to warm them up, and this will not have an adverse effect on the set of your sail.

When your are racing in very low temperatures, you will find that you can sail on with very little pain once you have passed the first stage of coldness and your fingers or toes have become dead. It is only when you have finished, and life gradually returns to your fingertips as they warm up slowly, that you feel a prickling and burning sensation which is hard to describe adequately. During this stage I have often seen really tough young men grimacing with pain and staring at their hands with tears in their eyes. This agony lasts for about a quarter of an hour, and anybody who has suffered it will do all he can to avoid a repetition.

PROTESTS

Frequently, some of those competing in a sailboard race are beginners who do not know the racing rules thoroughly. Equally, many boardsailors take a lenient view of rule infringements, such as minor collisions or being hindered, to avoid having to take the tiresome and distasteful step of making a protest. I feel, however, that the rules should be complied with, and that anybody who has broken a rule should be asked to make a 720° turn, even when the incident has not hindered or damaged the board that has been fouled or touched. When an incident occurs, and there is no dispute over which board has breached the rules, the 720° turn is undoubtedly the right and simplest method of penalizing the rule-breaker, while the right of way board should benefit by improving his position. In those cases where the boardsailors involved disagree, the only solution is to make a protest.

The exact position of a board on the water when a collision occurs cannot be fixed exactly, and both parties should therefore look immediately for witnesses who saw the whole incident and will be ready to make a statement.

If a mark has been touched in the process, the boardsailor should find out at once whether one of those on board the race officers' boat at the mark is prepared to act as a witness on his behalf. These race officials may consider wrongly that they have seen a board touch the mark, and the only hope then is to find several witnesses who were very close at hand, and saw clearly that this was not so. Such witnesses are often asked during the hearing to produce credible evidence to the effect that they were actually able to see exactly what occurred.

Generally the punishment for infringing a rule is disqualification which, when series racing, can be discarded as the worst result unless, as often is the case in major events, there is an additional rule in the sailing instructions stipulating that any disqualification must be included in the points total. The object of this is to enforce competitors to observe the rules more carefully.

Appendix 3 of the IYRU Racing Rules relates to alternative penalties that may be applied when a competitor has breached one of the right of way rules. It is, however, better to acknowledge a breach immediately it has occurred so that, after making a 720° turn, you can continue on your course with a clear conscience, rather than be disqualified as a result of a difficult protest on account of statements made by your opponent's witnesses.

It is no disgrace to be involved in a protest; problems that can be solved in

no other way arise again and again during races. Part IV of the racing rules gives full details about protests, disqualification and appeals.

When you are the person making the protest:

- If you consider that you are in the right after a collision or having been seriously hindered, you must immediately try to advise the other boardsailor that you intend to protest.
- If you have been involved in or witnessed an infringement of one of the right of way rules and intend to make a protest, you must immediately try to advise the other boardsailor.
- You can inform him by hailing 'Protest' or '720' to instruct him to make a 720° turn.
- If he does not acknowledge his fault by making a 720° turn, look for witnesses who saw the incident and could support your statement, even if it seems obvious to you that the protest could only be decided in your favour.
- Advise the officials on the committee boat when finishing that you are making a protest, and give them the sail number of the other board.
- On land, write down your protest, giving exact details of what occurred and a diagram of the incident.
- Quote the number of the rule or rules which you consider the other board has infringed.
- Deliver the signed protest to the race committee before the time limit stated, together with any fee required (in cash). The time limit is extended if you only become aware later that a rule has been breached (eg protest relating to measurement).
- Discuss the incident with your wit-

nesses to ensure that no minor contradictory evidence could cast doubts as to what actually occurred. Inform your witnesses when they will be required to give evidence.

When the protest is heard, the two parties attend (separately at first) and the details of the incident are established with the help of additional sketches and explanations. The witnesses called by both parties are questioned by the race committee, and must also answer questions put by the opposing party. When the race committee has gathered all the necessary information it withdraws to consider the protest, and the decision is communicated to the parties involved (in writing if so desired) as well as to the race officers.

An appeal against the decision may be made by the loser or any party involved (including the race committee itself), and the protest is then referred to the national authority solely on a question of interpretation of rules, and not with a view to establishing what actually occurred.

If a protest is decided in favour of the boardsailor making the protest, the fee paid is refunded.

When a protest is made against you:
• If you collide with or seriously hinder someone during a race and have clearly breached a right of way rule, avoid disqualification by acknowledging your infringement and make a 720° turn.
• If the incident is not straightforward, the other board fails to shout 'Protest' or '720' as he should, use this omission later as an argument as to why the protest should not be heard.
• If you are convinced that you are in the right, ignore your opponent's instruction to make a 720° turn.
• Make a mental note of the sail numbers of witnesses who could have seen exactly what happened.
• When finishing, ask whether the boardsailor has notified the race officers that he is making a protest.
• Immediately you land, check the relevant racing rule carefully.
• Discuss the incident with all the boardsailors involved (except the protester) to see if other points can be put forward in your favour.
• Try to give the protesting boardsailor the impression that you think your case in hopeless. He should be sure of his case when presenting it to the race committee, but must not be forewarned of your interpretation of the rules and the arguments you will be putting forward because he would then be able to refute them when putting his own case.
• Establish exactly what occurred with your witnesses, so that no contradictions arise when the race committee hears the case.
• Try to discover what the protesting boardsailor's statement will be so that, during the hearing, you can bring forward conflicting points and so cast doubt on the credibility of the other party by exposing contradictions.
• Concentrate your description of the incident on the actual facts of the case and, when possible, base your defence on the racing rules.
• Be brief and factual. Chatter, or digressing from the point or indulging in an emotional outburst only give the impression that you are unsure of your case.

Even a protest that appears to be hopeless at first sight can be won if you study the rules really carefully, because there are exceptions to almost every rule. These exceptions apply in particular circumstances, and the rule will not then have been infringed. One example of this is when a protest is made under rule 36 (Port tack keeps clear of the starboard tack).

• Rule 35 : *When one yacht is required to keep clear of another, the right of way yacht shall not so alter course as to prevent the other yacht from keeping clear; or so as to obstruct her while she is keeping clear . . .*

If you can produce witnesses who confirm that the right of way board did alter course in this way you could avoid disqualification.

Unless the sailing instructions specify otherwise, a competitor who has started and finished may not be disqualified from the race without a hearing. The race committee cannot therefore simply disqualify a boardsailor as a result of receiving information that he has infringed a rule, but must follow virtually the same procedure as a protesting competitor and call a hearing.

REFRESHMENT

The sport of boardsailing uses muscles and nerves to the full. During a series, especially when it is sailed in strong winds, the demands made on the neuro-muscular system are so great that signs of fatigue appear in spite of hard training to increase strength and performance.

A well-balanced diet helps the boardsailor to remain fully active for a longer period. The body's energy requirement increases during training as well, but the answer is not suddenly to alter eating habits or to have much larger meals. It is more effective to eat protein and fat-enriched foods with a view to speeding up muscle formation. Some vitamins also increase reserves of strength, and discourage or delay onset of muscular fatigue. Vitamin C helps to neutralize the effects of lactic acid; this forms in stressed muscles and, in excess, causes weakness. Vitamins B6 and B12 also have an antitoxic effect, while B6 strengthens heart muscles as well. These vitamins are already present in well-balanced meals, but can be supplemented by pills if necessary. Avoid taking too many vitamins; an excess can cause poisoning.

All the internationally recognized boardsailing classes are divided into weight groups, and your weight therefore has to be considered. Lighter boardsailors always have the advantage, except when the wind is blowing above Force 6, and it is therefore preferable to be one of the lightest in you weight group. However, if you take off a few pounds of weight by doing some hard training, you will be more mobile and your feeling of well-being will be greater than if you fatten yourself up to squeeze into the next higher weight group. In any case you lose weight during a race, and consequently will soon find that you are under the weight limit again. One possibility open to you, and it has happened, is to fill one or both of your boardsailing boots full of water surreptitiously before being weighed on land . . .

In order to provide the extra energy needed when taking part in one or more races, eat a good meal three hours before the first start at the latest. It should be a varied but not too heavy meal, and fried or fatty foods are

unsuitable. Do not drink more than a quarter of a litre of fluid while eating, but you can follow this with fresh fruit juice at intervals during the period before the race.

You may be allowed to leave something on board the boat at the finish line, and can then refresh yourself between races with a mixture of fresh fruit juice and glucose in half a litre or more of flat mineral water or, when the temperature is low, with glucose and warm or hot tea. A good broth with an egg in it, eaten in some suitable spot on shore, is a particularly quick way of providing fresh energy for a freezing body. Avoid drinks laced with alcohol because alcohol does not warm the body and merely affects the nervous system; you do not then notice how cold you are, and your ability to concentrate and to coordinate your movements will certainly deteriorate in the race that follows.

If you have to provide for yourself on the water between races, take some glucose tablets with you; they too delay the onset of fatigue and will help you to concentrate when the time comes to start the next race.

Marathon racing

When taking part in a marathon race, which may be as long as 20 nautical miles, the demands on man and material are considerably greater than when racing round a triangular Olympic course, and very thorough preparation is therefore essential.

The human body is rarely accustomed to being under stress for periods of longer than one hour: both the ability to concentrate and physical fitness decrease gradually after this time has elapsed. You may be unable to train in the area where the race is to be run, and you should then find out how long the course will be and the maximum time that it will take to cover it so that you can train in local waters round a course of comparable length, preferably with approximately the same proportion of beating, reaching and running.

If you have no-one to train with, you can race against the clock to force yourself to make use of every method of increasing speed.

Make sure before the race that you know exactly what the course is, and that you could sail round it correctly even if you found yourself in the lead. On many an occasion a boardsailor has not paid proper attention at the skippers' meeting before a long race, and then found himself leading without knowing where the next mark of the course is laid. If the marks cannot be seen from the shore, you will need to find landmarks which will help you to locate them. When in unknown waters, and unable to sail the whole course before the race, you have to rely on sketches or verbal information, and must be sure that no confusion over the marks can arise.

Before you start a marathon race, find out whether the water is very shallow anywhere on or near the course so that you are forewarned and will react correctly the first time that you run aground. Try to obtain a weather forecast and look at a weather map to find out what major wind shifts are expected and whether there are likely to be thunder squalls, especially if the course includes a very long beat.

The question of what equipment to take with you must be carefully considered. I recommend you always to take a harness, even if the wind seems unlikely to exceed Force 4. Whether on the coast or inland, the weather can change greatly within a period of hours.

When the race will last longer than two hours, carry half a litre of orange juice and glucose in a bottle attached either to your body or to the boom so that you can refresh and revitalize yourself with a drink, either while you

are hanging in the harness if the wind is fresh, or when you are on the run in light winds.

The size of your sail will depend on the average wind speed expected. The downhaul and kicking strap should be led in such a way that, if the wind becomes too strong, you can release them both and push the part of the mast sleeve beneath the boom up about 50–80 cm to reduce the area of the sail.

When the race starts with a long broad reach or run, and you will be crossing the starting line on the same

Starting a long-distance race off Waikiki, Hawaii.

point of sailing, you may prefer to sail without a daggerboard. You can then fill the daggerboard slot from beneath with a piece of expanded foam to prevent the famous daggerboard slot fountain, which considerably reduces board speed, from spouting upwards into your face. When you reach the mark the foam is pushed out as you insert the daggerboard.

The course may take you around natural obstructions such as islands or past large anchored ships, and you have to avoid the area where you would be blanketed, and where the wind is turbulent and eddies occur. These areas extend approximately three times the height of the obstruction to windard and six times its height to leeward.

When the wind is blowing from a direction that enables you to fetch the first mark from the starting line without having to go about, the best position on the starting line is at the end that is closer to the first mark. However, when this position is at the leeward end of the line, the sailboards to windward benefit sooner from fresher gusts than those to leeward, and not only do they make up the deficit but can then blanket the leeward boards. The decision whether to start at the lee end of the line or not depends on whether you are sure you will be able to avoid being blanketed by boards to windward.

It is relatively rare for boards to start on a run; generally this occurs only when, regardless of wind direction, the time taken to complete the course is compared with the times of earlier races over that particular course. With a running start and a starting line that is not quite at right angles to the wind direction, the side that is further to leeward is preferable, the advantage gained being the difference in distance to leeward between the two ends of the line. Approach the start very cautiously during the last few minutes because there is no way to reduce the speed at which you drift downwind when you are all bunched together. After crossing the line, move to one side to avoid being blanketed by following boards; because the fleet will not spread out during the run and there is bound to be severe crowding at the first mark, the side to which you move after the start should be that which will give you the inside berth at the mark.

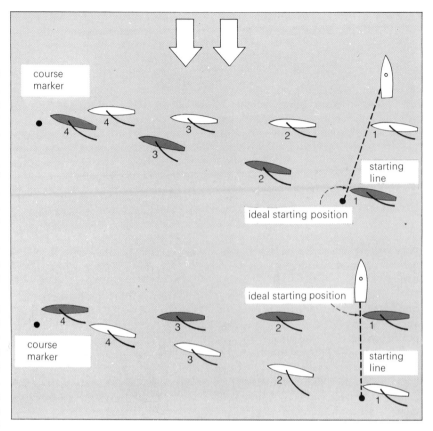

Starting when the first mark can be fetched without tacking.

5 Training on dry land

Whatever the weather conditions, boardsailing is a strenuous sport that makes great demands on strength, concentration and fitness, and requires good coordination. It is not just a question of preparing the sailboard and trimming the sail for maximum performance; the boardsailor himself must be absolutely physically fit.

You need to concentrate mainly on tactics and sailing technique during a hard-fought race, and your physical responses must be automatic. Any sign of fatigue, cramp or muscular pain affects a boardsailor's performance so much that he is neither able to keep the board moving at full speed, nor use the right tactics and strategy. Furthermore his will to win diminishes as his physical condition deteriorates.

You need to build up your general physique, both by training thoroughly on the water and by doing appropriate exercises on land, if you are to be fit enough to race in all weathers, even when conditions are hard.

Be sure that you are healthy before you begin increasing your strength and improving your physical condition by gradually making exercises more strenuous. A medical check-up before starting a training programme is particularly advisable if you are not already involved in an active sport and physical training.

The increase in the demands made on your neuro-muscular and circulatory systems must be very gradual to allow time for your body to respond. Be careful not to overstrain yourself, or overstretch the joints, especially when weight training. Ligaments and tendons are more easily damaged than muscles during training.

Cross-country running is an easy way to start to get into shape, and is a good base on which to build a programme of appropriate exercises. Running regularly and doing gymnastics prepares the body for greater loads, and the speed and output can gradually be increased. The results soon become apparent in greater freedom of movement, and feeling of well-being.

It is more important to train regularly than to make intermittent strenuous efforts. Stiffness is overcome more effectively by continuing with light training, and is a sign that the demands made on your body as you train are showing a positive improvement in performance.

Many boardsailors enjoy other sports as well, and continuing to take part in these activities will help to keep them fit. Tennis, squash, skiing and skateboarding are sports which complement boardsailing well because you need to be fitter for them than for boardsailing, and they also speed up your reactions and improve your neuro-muscular coordination. Ball games, in particular, help reactions, while sports such as skiing and skateboarding, when locomotion involves the use of apparatus, improve balance and the ability to respond to changing the position of the body's centre of gravity.

There is no doubt that it helps to pursue a strenuous sport, or some activity that keeps you generally fit, because this compensates for what is mainly a static load when boardsailing. If you find that you still become fatigued in stronger winds, you should follow a special training programme.

To improve fitness

Physical limitations during a race usually result from overloading specific muscles, and the aim when training, therefore is, to raise these limits by improving the performance of particular parts of your body. The forearms are the first to cause problems. The effort of continuously holding the boom is a static load (which cannot always be relieved by using a harness), calling for muscles that are well supplied with blood and able to endure long periods of tension. When training at home you can achieve good results at small cost by simulating the muscular work required when boardsailing.

After doing some simple warm-up exercises, hang on a tube until the first signs of fatigue appear in you forearms; then relax your stressed muscles and repeat the exercise several times. The tube, the diameter of which should be roughly equal to that of the boom, should be at such a height that you just cannot sit on the floor when your arms are at full stretch. You can either fix the tube as a horizontal bar in a door frame, or hang it from ropes attached to a stepladder or some other places of suitable height. To make your hanging position more efficient by matching it to your position on the sailboard, you can brace your feet against some object so that the pull does not come vertically downwards but is transmitted sideways to your leg and arm muscles. As well as the purely isometric (muscular tension without joint movement) load on your arms, you can do exercises such as pull-ups while hanging in this position, keeping your muscles under strain and bending your elbows to varying degrees until signs of fatigue appear. The strength of your fingers will be increased if the tube is not too easy to grip, and you can make it even more slippery by smearing it with vaseline.

After several weeks training, your muscles should be able to stay under stress for about 5–10 minutes, depending on how hard it is to grip the tube, while the rest intervals become progressively shorter. You can increase the time that you can hold on like this if you try to vary the load on your muscles by relaxing your grip and altering the pressure points on your hands while maintaining the same arm position.

Another area that gives trouble is where great strains are put on the muscles between your seat and your shoulders. When boardsailing, their job is to keep the body bent at a certain angle, and to prevent it from collapsing. The tube that simulates the boom is of only limited help because insufficient load is applied to your bent hips to strengthen the muscles and improve their performance. To stimulate the forces involved, stand in front of a chair seat with your feet placed so that your bent head is just over the front edge; then lift the chair up by the sides until you are standing upright. Bend and straighten your hips repeatedly, and then remain static in various positions until signs of fatigue appear.

The third set of muscles that are frequently overstressed and become tired are those in the lower leg; bracing your feet can cause pain and cramp in the calves, even in light airs. As side pressure increases so does the strain on your feet, which are not always placed in a normal position when they are transmitting the driving force developed by the rig to the board.

No apparatus is needed for calf strengthening exercises; just stand on your toes and hold this position for about half a minute, then lower the

To increase strength

heels and repeat the exercise several times. You can increase the load by standing in a doorway, pushing downwards with your hands braced against the top of the frame while you are standing on your toes. As well as working on this isometric exercise, movement can be encouraged by repeatedly flexing and extending the ankles.

With all these exercises, it is not the intensity with which you do them but regularity and a gradual increase of effort that are most effective. They only take a few minutes, and should therefore be done twice daily if possible, morning and evening.

Strengthening apparatus, such as spring dumbells which are held under tension with one hand, or a spherical shell with a plastic ball which revolves inside, the rate of revolution being kept constant or increased by a circular movement of the wrist, can also be used for forearms. Frequent use of either of these enables forearm and finger muscles to support a considerably increased static load.

Performance in strong winds can be improved by following a programme designed to increase general strength, with greater attention being paid to the particularly highly stressed forearm, back and calf muscles. A balanced training programme strengthens all other muscles as well, and is best followed under the supervision of a sports instructor in a suitably equipped sports hall. One example is interval training, when individual muscles are exercised in turn at regular intervals of about 20–60 seconds, each exercise being followed by a pause of similar duration before the next is started. Ten to twelve exercises are repeated several times, and the improvement in performance results not only from the length of time that the muscles are stressed but from the rhythmic pattern of alternating effort with rest. A sequence of exercises for interval training could be as follows:

- Skipping.
- Balance sitting.
- Hip circling.
- Dorsal extension, throwing up and catching a medicine ball in the prone position.

- Jumping sideways back and forth over a bench about 50 cm high.
- Hanging with arms bent on a parallel bar that is forehead high.
- Rhythmic bending and stretching on wall bars, rising as the distance between arms and legs is increased

Skipping.

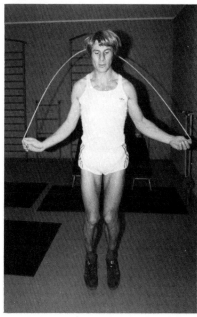

one bar at a time, and then lowering the body as the distance between them is reduced again.

- Press-ups.
- Bending your knees with your heels on the floor, followed by a stretch jump.
- Pull-ups (chin-to-bar).
- Standing with legs astride and throwing up and catching a medicine ball with both arms.
- Stand with legs astride and straight knees, bending the whole trunk down over alternate legs.

Each exercise is performed continuously for a period of, say, 30 seconds, followed by 30 seconds of rest during which the apparatus is changed. After each sequence of exercises, an extra five minutes rest is

Hip circling.

Throwing up a medicine ball.

Balance sitting.

Jumping over a bench.

Balance hanging.

Wall bar exercise.

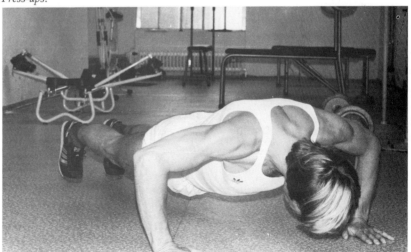

Press-ups.

Pull-ups.

allowed, but initially one sequence is usually enough. The frequency of the exercises should not be increased before a marked increase in strength has been achieved.

Broadly speaking, greater endurance results from repeating one exercise frequently without using too much effort, whereas momentary strength results from performing an exercise less often but with maximum effort. For boardsailing, which makes particular demands on individual muscles that are stressed for long periods, the accent should be on frequent repetition of exercises and relatively little resistance to pulling and lifting actions.

A person's ability to sail in strong winds is not measured by strength alone but by his performance relative to his weight. By this I mean how strong he is compared to each kilo of his body weight, for example, how many press-ups or chins he can do. This is why someone with a light but strong physique has the advantage over a heavier person whose strength is only average.

All these suggestions and tips, and all this advice may sound as though they promise success, but I must now destroy my readers' illusions. No one can learn to race successfully just by reading theory and making practical preparations. Regular racing alone teaches a sailor how to make use of the weather and all the other factors that affect the course of a race.

The advice I have given stems from what I have learnt and from my experiences in about 400 sailboard races. Part is my own opinion, but the rest is based on long-established theory which has been proved when racing sailing boats, but which is equally valid for sailboards. And yet, every time I race I learn more tricks, and the finer points help me to stay successful.

One essential attribute for success is confidence; you must be sufficiently confident of your ability to hold on to a good position right up to the finish. This is not the time to be nervous or unsure. Your determination to win the race must persist right to the finish if all your intensive training and carefully made preparations are to be rewarded with a good result.

Trunk bending.

Presentation of prizes.

Flag signals made during a race

Red flag		all course marks to be left to port
Green flag		all course marks to be left to starboard
Flag P (the Blue Peter)		preparatory signal (three or, more often, five minutes before the starting signal)
Flag Y		personal buoyancy must be worn
Flag I		round the ends rule in force
Flag X		individual recall
First substitute		general recall